NARROW GAUGE AND INDUSTRIAL RAILWAYS

THE LATE 1940s TO LATE 1960s

Brian Reading and Ian Reading

AMBERLEY

First published 2023

Amberley Publishing
The Hill, Stroud
Gloucestershire, GL5 4EP

www.amberley-books.com

Copyright © Brian Reading and Ian Reading, 2023

The right of Brian Reading and Ian Reading to
be identified as the Authors of this work has
been asserted in accordance with the Copyrights,
Designs and Patents Act 1988.

ISBN 978 1 3981 0012 1 (print)
ISBN 978 1 3981 0013 8 (ebook)

British Library Cataloguing in Publication Data.
A catalogue record for this book is available from
the British Library.

Typesetting by SJmagic DESIGN SERVICES, India.
Printed in Great Britain.

Introduction

The 1950s and 1960s was an era of post-war renewal and change. Car ownership was increasing, road haulage costs were reducing and Britain's traditional heavy industries were struggling against overseas competition. For the small engines that connected local communities, moved minerals and tirelessly shunted near factories, the curtain was gradually falling. Railway preservation groups formed and heroically began to protect at least some of our heritage from scrap. As improving living standards enabled a growing leisure economy, an inspiring possibility began to emerge. Steam railways could become a destination and not merely a means to travel. By attracting visitors, railways could bring spending into the communities that they once served. Across the country, dedicated volunteers worked tirelessly so that characterful steam locomotives that were once engines of heavy industry could find a new role as engines of the tourism industry.

With pictures and recollections, we tour twelve of Britain's most interesting narrow gauge and industrial railways. Between 1955 and 1967, we see some of our country's oldest, newest and most charming engines at work.

On the Isle of Man, in the early 1960s, Indian red 1873-vintage Manx Peacocks were roaming over 46 miles, reaching Peel in the west and Ramsey in the north. At Corby, after thirty years of growth, in the mid-1960s steelmaking was reaching its peak. Britain's most powerful industrial steam locomotives, unfairly known as the 'Uglies', are pictured working side by side with their Manning Wardle ancestors to feed the furnaces' insatiable appetite for iron ore. Open cast mining of a completely different kind took place on North Norfolk's Sandringham Sands. Hard at work near Middleton Towers, we see Simplex locomotives helping to extract high quality glass making sand. The nearby Wissington Light Railway helped give birth to a factory that would become Europe's largest sugar beet processing plant. Pictured in the 1950s and 1960s, axle deep in grass and wildflowers, *Hayle* and *Newcastle* seem to know their way across the fens. A 1963 visit to Richard Garrett Engineering at Leiston glimpses *Sirapite*, reminiscent of a traction engine on rails. At Sittingbourne, the Bowater's railway was operating twenty-four hours a day. Working around the enormous paper mill, we see *Unique*, the first of Bagnall's many fireless locomotives and 0-4-4-0T *Monarch*, the last and one of the largest narrow gauge industrial steam engines built for service in the UK.

A tour of Wales begins with the Vale of Rheidol before moving inland to glimpse the Welshpool & Llanfair Light Railway. In the 1960s, quarries were closing and the slate boom was a distant memory. Built before 2-foot gauge locomotives could operate over long distances, the 1848 Padarn Railway used ingenious transporter wagons to move slate from quarry to port. Serving the largest slate mine in the world, *Blanche* and *Linda* are pictured on the nearby Penrhyn Quarry Railway. A *c.* 1955 visit captures the Talyllyn, newly saved as the world's first volunteer-run heritage railway.

Our tour concludes with the world's oldest independent railway company, the Festiniog. Its gently sloping route was brilliantly engineered by James Spooner, whose family went on to contribute to the Padarn, Penrhyn Quarry, and the Talyllyn railways. A sequence of pictures taken during the early years of preservation catches *Linda* in the sun, rescued from the Penrhyn Quarry Railway, as a gleaming symbol of hope for the future of steam heritage railways.

Finally, we would like to thank railway historians Richard Adderson, David Pearce and Frank Cooper for their generous assistance, Catriona and Kathleen for their help with research and proofing, and the Amberley team for their support and encouragement.

Isle of Man Railway
3-foot gauge
Opened with steam 1873, partly operational today

Dinorwic Quarries (Padarn) Railway
1-foot 10¾ inch & 4-foot gauge
Steam from 1848, closed 1961

Penrhyn Quarry Railway
1-foot 10¾ inch gauge
Opened with steam 1878, closed 1962

Festiniog Railway
1-foot 11½ inch gauge
Steam from 1864, heritage railway today

Talyllyn Railway
2-foot 3-inch gauge
Opened with steam 1865, heritage railway today

Vale of Rheidol Railway
1-foot 11¾ inch gauge
Opened with steam 1902, heritage railway today

Welshpool & Llanfair Railway
2-foot 6-inch gauge
Opened with steam 1903, heritage railway today

1

10
9
12
11
7
8
2

3
4

5

6

Stewarts & Lloyds Minerals Corby
Standard gauge
Steam from *c.*1910, closed 1980

Middleton Towers & Leziate Works
1-foot 11½ inch gauge
Internal combustion from 1919, closed 1977

Wissington Light Railway
Standard gauge
Opened with steam *c.*1906, closed 1981

Richard Garrett Engineering Leiston Works
Standard gauge
Steam from 1929, heritage railway today

Bowater's Railway
2-foot 6-inch gauge
Steam from 1905, heritage railway today

Isle of Man Railway

For more than 140 years, the Isle of Man has been home to a charming fleet of Beyer Peacock tank locomotives. Today, the nationalised 15-mile route from Douglas to Port Erin continues to be the longest narrow gauge line in Britain to use its original steam engines. In the early 1960s, the Isle of Man Railway (IMR) was still a private company and the 3-foot gauge Manx Peacocks roamed over 46 miles, reaching Peel in the west and Ramsey in the north.

The IMR was formed as a company in 1870 and by 1873 had opened a line from Douglas to Peel. A line from Douglas to Port Erin was added a year later in 1874. By 1879, the Manx Northern Railway Company (MNR) had opened a route from Ramsey south to connect at St John's with the IMR Douglas to Peel line. The Foxdale Railway was added in 1885 to link the lead mines south of St John's over the MNR to the port at Ramsey. The IMR purchased steam locomotives exclusively from Beyer Peacock. Its first three locomotives, *Sutherland*, *Derby* and *Pender*, were delivered in 1873 with *Loch* and *Mona* following in 1874 and *Peveril* in 1875. Though often associated with the Isle of Man, the 2-4-0T design was very similar to Beyer Peacock's Norwegian Railways Class IV 2-4-0T of 1866 and bore at least a family resemblance to the Metropolitan Railway Class A 4-4-0T of 1864. In contrast, the MNR had a more varied taste in locomotives. Its first two 2-4-0T locomotives, *Ramsey* and *Northern*, delivered by Sharp, Stewart & Co. in 1880, were only moderately successful. For its third locomotive the MNR followed the IMR to Beyer Peacock and purchased 2-4-0T *Thornhill* in 1880. Mineral traffic on the steep line to Foxdale required an 0-6-0T and for this, the MNR turned to Dübs & Co. from whom they purchased *Caledonia* in 1885. By the early 1900s the 1893 Manx Electric Railway was competing for traffic from Douglas to Ramsey and the Foxdale lead mines were facing closure. In 1904, the struggling MNR was taken over by the IMR. The IMR continued its relationship with Beyer Peacock adding *Tynwald* in 1880, *Fenella* in 1894 and *Douglas* in 1896. *G. H. Wood* and *Maitland* of 1905 were supplied with larger boilers, an upgrade that was subsequently retrofitted to some of the earlier engines. *Hutchinson* and *Kissack* followed in 1908 and 1910. The final and largest evolution of the Beyer Peacock design *Mannin* was delivered in 1926.

With a gradual loss of freight to road transport, seasonal tourism kept trains busy during summer months. By 1965 though, the IMR could struggle on no more. Under Archibald Kennedy, the Marquess of Ailsa, the IMR reopened in 1967. Routes to Peel and Ramsey were sadly closed in 1968. In 1978, the IMR was nationalised under the Isle of Man Department of Infrastructure. Thanks to the lobbying and active support of the Isle of Man Steam Railway Supporters' Association, the IMR has survived into what is today one of the islands leading tourist attractions. Though the MNR's two locomotives *Ramsey* and *Northern* were scrapped by 1923, *Caledonia* and *Thornhill* have been preserved. From the IMR's fleet, only *Derby* has been lost to scrap. All of the other Manx Peacocks have survived in museums, private collections or are still running. Though changed, sheds and many parts of the stations at Douglas and Port Erin remain. To the delight of enthusiasts and tourists, on the picturesque Isle of Man, the Manx Peacock continues to charm.

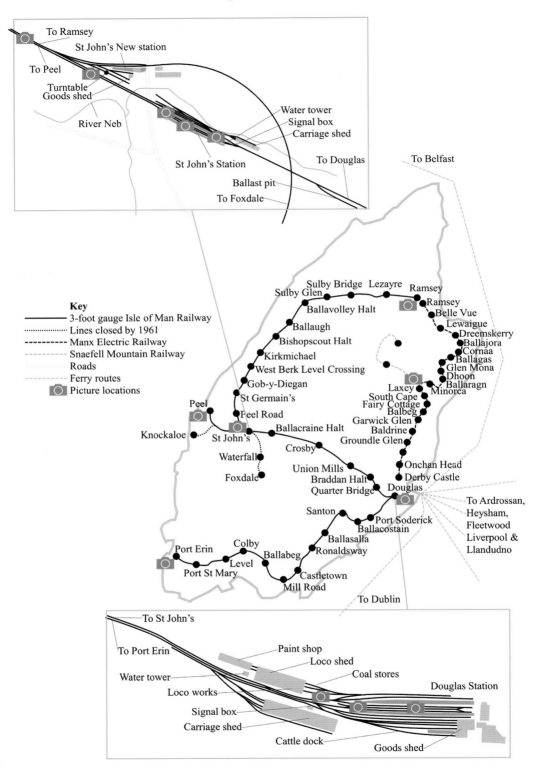

Fleetwood *c.* 1960, *TSS Mona's Isle*, one of the beautiful turbine steamers operated by the Isle of Man Steam Packet Co., leaves for Douglas. Though the four-hour crossing was sometimes rough, the vessels were comfortable, with super catering and nice restaurants. Seasonal schedules included routes from Liverpool, Fleetwood, Belfast, Dublin, Ardrossan, Heysham and Llandudno. One of the six sisters, 2,491-ton *TSS Mona's Isle*, was built by Cammell Laird in 1950 and sadly scrapped in 1980.

No. 8 *Fenella* arrives at Douglas in 1961 with a merged service from Peel and Ramsey. For a narrow gauge station, Douglas was quite an imposing terminus, with wide platforms and generous canopies. The station served routes to Ramsey, Peel and Port Erin. The leading coach, No. F.19, was supplied by Brown Marshalls & Co. in 1894 and sadly one of many lost to fire in 1976.

Holidaymakers hurry down the platform at Douglas in this 1962 picture. 2-4-0T No. 8 *Fenella* uses the engine release road to run round its train. No. 8 was built in 1894 by Beyer Peacock as works No. 3610, and named after a character in Sir Walter Scott's novel *Peveril of the Peak*. Originally supplied with one of the earlier small boilers, a unique 160 psi boiler with a larger 2-foot 11-inch diameter was fitted in 1936.

No. 16 *Mannin* taking advantage of the primitive coaling facilities on a wet day at Douglas in 1962. Baskets of coal on the raised platform were moved by wheelbarrow from the stockpile beside the shed in the distance. Built with a recognisably different cab shape, *Mannin* was the last and most powerful of the 2-4-0T Manx Peacocks. Completed in 1926 as Beyer Peacock works No. 6296, she had large 12-inch bore cylinders and a 3-foot 6-inch diameter 180 psi boiler.

A 1961 view from the end of the platform at Douglas, looking towards the carriage shed. 2-4-0T No. 13 *Kissack* waits for its next duty. Although the water crane, signal box, and much of the station remain, the carriage shed has today been replaced by a car park, bus depot and supermarket.

Douglas 1962, No. 14 *Thornhill* waits for its departure time. The timber stage beside the water crane was used to accommodate wicker baskets of coal. Though parts of the station remain in use today, sadly the generous canopies and the platform on the right have been removed. In the distance on the right, the goods depot has now been redeveloped as a bus and car park.

No. 14 *Thornhill* poses by neatly piled coal near Douglas shed. Named after Thornhill House, the Chairman's residence, she was built for the Manx Northern Railway (MNR) in 1880 by Beyer Peacock as works No. 2028. Unique among the Manx 2-4-0T locomotives, *Thornhill* retained many original features including Salter safety valves and a sloping smokebox front. Pictured in 1962, she was withdrawn with boiler problems in 1963. No. 14 is currently preserved in private ownership.

St John's 1962, looking south-east towards the water tower and signal box at the Douglas end of the station. The line from Douglas diverged at St John's with routes heading west to Peel and north to Ramsey. The Foxdale branch, which closed to freight in 1960, crosses the Douglas line and runs on an embankment in the distance. Released from its arriving train, No. 5 *Mona* waits on the left with its safety valves impatiently blowing. No. 8 *Fenella* leaves for Douglas with the merged services from Peel and Ramsey.

Off peak trains from Douglas to Ramsey and Peel were often combined as far as St John's. Pictured in 1962, *Kissack* prepares to depart from St John's with the Peel portion of the service from Douglas. No. 13 was built by Beyer Peacock in 1910 as works No. 5382. She was named in honour of Isle of Man Railway (IMR) Company Director Edward Thomas Kissack.

St John's 1962, No. 13 *Kissack* departs for Peel. Looking south-east, the bridge in the distance carries the recently disused Foxdale branch over the main line to Douglas. An oil can is positioned below the smokebox door to keep warm near the valve chests, a practice adopted by many of the Manx drivers.

No. 8 *Fenella* waits with the Ramsey portion of the service from Douglas. St John's station opened with the IMR Douglas to Peel line in 1873. In 1879 the site was expanded with the MNR route to Ramsey, initially with separate and then merged stations. As the hub of the island's railways, St John's became known as the Manx Crewe. Advertising posters form a colourful 1962 backdrop. Phil Moss is playing at the Villa Marina, Manx National Sheepdog Trials, Beer, and, as the picture confirms, colour comes out best on Kodak film!

St John's 1961, No.8 *Fenella* departs for Ramsey. Coach No. F.23 dates from 1896 and was built by the Metropolitan Carriage & Wagon Co. The trees in the background mark the location of what was once the short-lived St John's New station, added by the MNR in 1884. The Foxdale branch opened in 1886 and ran beyond the hotel on the right.

St John's station looking north-east towards the spire of the Royal Chapel of St John the Baptist, 1962.
Built by the Metropolitan Carriage & Wagon Co. in 1889, No. M.49 was one of seventy-eight two-plank
wagons operated on the Isle of Man. Originally conceived for ballast, they were versatile and used for many
applications. Safety chains and Norwegian-style couplings were used throughout the railway. Seldom turned,
locomotives and wagon couplings were fitted with chopper hooks only on the end pointing towards Douglas.

Looking east from a vantage point near the western end of St John's, 1961. The former MNR New station was
located beyond the good shed. In the foreground, the only turntable on the railway was used to turn coaches to
help them weather evenly on both sides. The Ransomes & Rapier turntable was acquired from the West Clare
Railway in Ireland and installed in 1925.

Left: The race is on! Trains for Ramsey and Peel left St John's together and sped side by side until the lines diverged. Viewed from the Peel train, on this occasion, Ramsey-bound *Fenella* may be conceding victory. Pictured in 1962, the routes to Peel and Ramsey sadly closed in 1968. Fortunately, No. 8 *Fenella* is preserved in running condition.

Below: Peel 1962, No. 13 *Kissack* is being prepared for the run to Douglas. Like many of its shed mates, *Kissack* is fitted with Ross pop safety valves in place of the original Salter spring type. No. 13 retains an original taper profile chimney. *Kissack* is preserved and maintained in running condition on the Isle of Man.

Peel 1962, No. 5 *Mona* joins No. 13 *Kissack* to double-head the late afternoon summer service to Douglas. As passengers board, the driver strolls forward to join his locomotive. When the service reaches St John's, the leading engine will move to the rear of the train for the run to Douglas. This configuration enabled engine release at Douglas and helped more of the train to be beside the platform. Opened in 1873, Peel station finally closed to passengers in 1968. Some of the station buildings remain as part of the House of Mannanan museum.

No. 11 *Maitland* approaches Ramsey with a train from Douglas. No. 11 was built by Beyer Peacock in 1905 (works No. 4663) and received a new boiler with Ross pop safety valves in 1935. Pictured in 1962, she was named after Dalrymple Maitland, Chairman of the IMR. Maitland was also a board member for the Isle of Man Steam Packet Company, and the Isle of Man Bank, and served as Speaker of the House of Keys. No. 11 is preserved and under restoration.

No. 5 *Mona* rests behind the goods shed at Ramsey. *Mona* was delivered by Beyer Peacock as works No. 1417 in 1874. Supplied with slightly larger side tanks than earlier locomotives, she was rebuilt with a larger diameter boiler in 1911. No. 5 was named after Mona's Isle, the Latin name for the Isle of Man. Pictured in 1962, she was withdrawn in 1969, privately purchased in 1978 and is currently unrestored.

Ramsey station and engine shed in 1962. One or two locomotives were out-stationed at Ramsey and Peel to work early morning services to Douglas. Ramsey was opened in 1879 as the terminus of the MNR, the single-storey Italianate building was unique on the island's railway system. Sadly, few traces of the station remain today. Closed to passengers in 1968, the site was redeveloped in 1978 for the Ramsey Bakery.

In the 1960s, freight was still thriving on the island's railways, often with mixed passenger and goods trains. A typical covered van waits beside the engine shed at Ramsey. Pictured in 1962, No. G.5 was built by the Ashbury Carriage & Iron Co. in 1877 and survived in service until 1965. The advertising sign encourages travellers to insure with the Ocean Accident & Guarantee Corporation.

Port Erin station in 1962 with both platforms still in use. The step and crossing on the platforms was an unusual feature of the station. Of the IMR's three main routes only the line from Douglas to Port Erin survives as a heritage railway. The station opened in 1874 and was expanded and updated in the early 1900s. Station buildings, engine shed, the left-hand platform and a simplified track layout remain in use today. A museum was opened near the station in 1975.

Port Erin 1962, No. 10 *G. H. Wood* pauses by the shed for boiler tube cleaning. No. 10 was one of the locomotives originally built with a larger boiler. She was delivered by Beyer Peacock as works No. 4662 in 1905 and named after IMR company secretary George Henry Wood. A seldom used rerailing screw-jack, carried by most of the island's locomotives, is visible on top of the side tank. No. 10 is currently preserved in running condition.

The largest of the island's 2-4-0T locomotives, No. 16 *Mannin* was long associated with the line to Port Erin. Mannin Ellan Vannin means Isle of Man in the Manx language. Former MNR van No. Gr.14 dates from 1897, and like many of the island's freight vehicles, was withdrawn in the 1960s and scrapped in the early 1970s. Pictured at Port Erin in 1962, No. 16 is preserved today with hopes that it will soon be restored to running condition.

Manx Electric Railway car No. 7 passes the Laxey goods shed *c.* 1962. No. 7 was originally built with a bow collector in 1894 and fitted with a trolley pole in 1898. After more than 125 years, she remains in service today. Originally powered by the railway's own power stations, the 550V DC tramway runs along the east coast from Douglas to Ramsey via Laxey. The double track of the 3-foot gauge tramway runs in the foreground. The 3-foot 6-inch gauge Snaefell Mountain Railway line runs in the background.

Laxey station *c.* 1962. Manx Electric Railway car No. 7 waits on the left while Snaefell Mountain Railway car No. 3 stands in line on the right. No. 3 was built by G. F. Milnes of Birkenhead and delivered in 1895. Hopkinson bow collectors continue to be used on the Snaefell line to cope with high winds on the climb to the exposed summit. The steepest parts of the route use a central Fell Rail system with gripper wheels to help with braking. No. 3 was sadly destroyed in a 2016 runaway incident near the summit.

Stewarts & Lloyds Minerals Corby

With a network of railways extending like roots into the ore field, and furnaces that glowed red in the night sky, Corby was once home to Europe's largest combined steelworks.

In the mid-1960s after thirty years of expansion, steel production at Corby was reaching its peak. A fleet of soot-coated yellow Hawthorn Leslie, Barclay and Hudswell Clarke tank locomotives tended the mills and furnaces. Coal and fuel oil arrived by rail and glowing pig iron was shunted between buildings. North of the works, from 1954, the Minerals Division operated from Pen Green shed. The Minerals Division maintained a green fleet described by its Locomotive Superintendent, Mr Bates, as the cleanest in the British Isles.

Corby stands on huge deposits of iron-rich sediments formed in shallow Jurassic seas. The town appeared in the Doomsday Book of 1086 as the iron-producing 'Manor of Corbei'. It was the enterprising Lloyd family, though, who catalysed industrial steel making at Corby. In 1698 religious intolerance drove Sampson Lloyd away from his Quaker family's ancestral home of Dolobran in Montgomeryshire. From a new base in Birmingham, Lloyd and his descendants built their wealth in the foundry and banking businesses. In 1859, Samuel Lloyd (III) started the steel tube maker Lloyd & Lloyd with his cousin. Ironstone exposed by railway cuttings near Gretton Brook was worked from 1851 and by 1880 Samuel had formed another company, Lloyds Ironstone, to mine and smelt near Corby. Glasgow-based Stewarts & Lloyds (S&L) was formed from the 1901 merger of Lloyd & Lloyd of Birmingham with Stewart & Menzies of Coatbridge. In 1919 Alfred Hickman Ltd of Bilston merged with Lloyds Ironstone, in 1922 Stewarts & Lloyds bought Alfred Hickman Ltd and by 1932 S&L was investing £3.2 million in a new and enormous steelworks at Corby. With an influx of workers from S&L's other plants, Corby became known as 'Little Scotland'. Production started in 1935, four years before the outbreak of the Second World War. In common with other steel producers, much of Corby's output supported the war effort. 2.5 million tons of steel formed into 275,000 miles of tube was delivered to war-related work. Projects included Pipe Lines Under The Ocean (PLUTO) and 15,000 miles of tube for beach defences. Pipe made at Corby for PLUTO was coiled onto a floating drum and unwound across the English Channel. More than 120 million gallons of fuel passed through the pipe to support Allied troops after the D-Day landing.

Output from the Open Hearth and Bessemer processes grew from 250,000 tons in 1935 to peaks of more than a million tons per year in the mid-1960s. As the steelworks grew, so did the demands for ore placed on the Minerals Division. As new quarries opened, routes were extended, often with track lifted and reused from older workings. In the mid-1960s, the more than 50 route-miles of the Mineral Division were worked by a fleet that traced its design heritage back to Manning Wardle. 0-6-0ST *Dolobran* was purchased by Lloyds Ironstone from Manning Wardle in 1910 and named after the Lloyd family ancestral home in Wales. With 16x22 inch cylinders and a raised firebox, *Dolobran* was an enlarged version of Manning Wardle's contractor's design. In *c.* 1912 Lloyds Ironstone purchased two slightly smaller Manning Wardle 0-6-0ST locomotives *Calettwr* and *Rhiwnant* that had been released from the Birmingham Corporation Elan Valley Reservoir project. *Rhyl* and *Rhondda* arrived in 1921 built to the same large design as *Dolobran*. When Manning Wardle closed in 1926, S&L purchased seven new locomotives from Kitson & Co. Delivered between 1933 and 1936, *Conway*, *Colwyn*, *Cardigan*, *Carnarvon*, *Criggion*, *Caerphilly*, and *Carmarthen* closely followed the design of *Dolobran*. Kitson & Co. closed in 1938 with their designs passing to Robert Stephenson & Hawthorns (RSH). S&L purchased a further five unnamed locomotives from RSH in 1940/41 that continued the successful *Dolobran* design. The large fleet of similar locomotives was used to ferry ore from quarries to the steelworks. Class members were also rotated out to more distant quarries including Glendon, to the south, and Buckminster, to the north of Corby.

With continued expansion in the 1950s, longer branches were built to connect the steelworks directly to quarries at Harringworth, Cowthick and Oakley. Heavy trains and longer routes created a requirement for larger and more powerful engines. The Mineral Division worked closely with RSH to specify No. 56, the first member of a class of nine that became the most powerful industrial steam locomotives operating in the UK.

From 1965, production at Corby largely moved over to the Basic Oxygen Steelmaking process. S&L was nationalised as part of British Steel in 1967 with production peaks staying above a million tons per year until the late 1970s. Although diesel locomotives arrived on the quarry lines in the late 1960s, a few steam locomotives were still in operation until *c.* 1971. During the 1970s, Corby struggled to maintain cost competitiveness with overseas steel makers and plants having access to higher yielding ore. With the loss of more than 6,000 jobs, British Steel closed the Corby works in 1980.

The sky no longer glows red above Corby. The furnaces have been demolished and quarries have been reclaimed for nature and recreation. The site of Pen Green shed has been redeveloped into a logistic centre and a 350 MW gas-fired power station. The steel works has been replaced with new industrial units. Buildings from the former S&L tube mill remain as part of Tata Steel and still produce 250,000 tons of welded steel tube each year. Supermarkets in Corby still sell more of Scotland's favourite Irn Bru than any other English town. A pub on Gretton Brook road has been named in memory of Samuel Lloyd. On preserved lines across the UK, many of the Mineral Division's locomotives are preserved and running. *Rhiwnant*, *Dolobran*, *Rhondda*, *Conway*, *Colwyn* and their classmate No. 54 are all safe in the care of dedicated enthusiasts. Five of the nine members of the 56 class have also been preserved with many in regular operation on heritage railways across the UK.

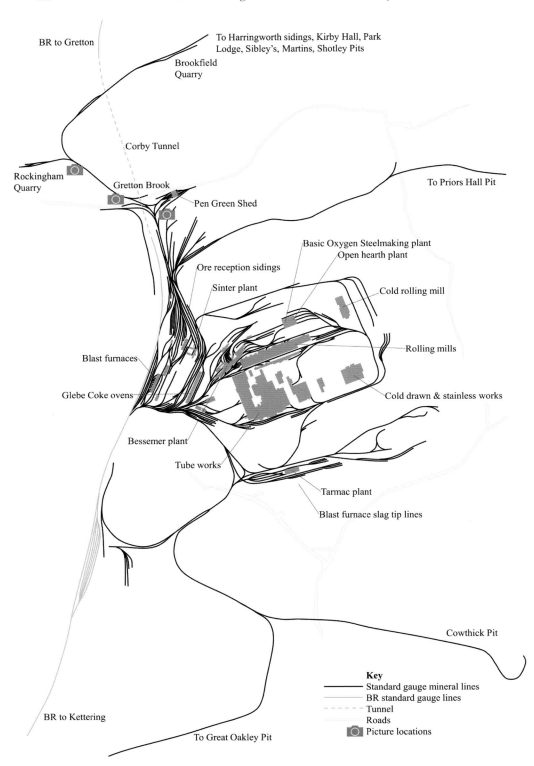

BR to Gretton

To Harringworth sidings, Kirby Hall, Park
Lodge, Sibley's, Martins, Shotley Pits

Brookfield
Quarry

Corby Tunnel

Rockingham
Quarry

Gretton Brook

Pen Green Shed

To Priors Hall Pit

Basic Oxygen Steelmaking plant
Open hearth plant

Ore reception sidings

Sinter plant

Cold rolling mill

Rolling mills

Blast furnaces

Glebe Coke ovens

Cold drawn & stainless works

Bessemer plant

Tube works

Tarmac plant

Blast furnace slag tip lines

Cowthick Pit

BR to Kettering

To Great Oakley Pit

Key
Standard gauge mineral lines
BR standard gauge lines
Tunnel
Roads
Picture locations

S&L Minerals No. 45 *Colwyn* heads south through Gretton Brook with an ironstone train bound for reception sidings near the main works. *Colwyn* was built by Kitson & Co. (works No. 5470) for S&L in 1933 as a continuation of an earlier Manning Wardle design. Pictured in the mid-1960s, No. 45 was moved to Storefield Quarries in 1969, before being withdrawn and preserved in 1971. In 1973, she starred in 'The Royal Train' episode of *Dad's Army*. Today she can be seen on the Northampton & Lamport Railway. Acknowledging the heritage of Lloyd family, *Colwyn* was one of several S&L locomotives named after Welsh towns. In the distance, just out of sight, No. 38 *Dolobran* helps at the rear of the train.

S&L No. 38 *Dolobran* helps at the rear as a train of ironstone hoppers rumbles south through Gretton Brook in the mid-1960s. *Dolobran* was built for S&L's predecessor, Lloyds Ironstone, by Manning Wardle (works No. 1762) in 1910. She was named after the Lloyd family ancestral home Dolobran Hall near Welshpool. No. 38 was withdrawn in 1968, preserved, and can be seen on the Great Central Railway.

During the 1960s the well maintained S&L rail system was extended to the north and south. S&L No. 35 heads south towards Gretton Brook with a plate layer's train in the mid-1960s. No. 35 was built by Manning Wardle (works No. 1317) in 1895 for the Elan Valley Reservoir project. It was purchased alongside No. 34 by Lloyds Ironstone in 1912. Nos 34 and 35 lacked the raised firebox of S&L's other similar Manning Wardle designed locomotives and could be recognised by their prominent dome covers. Named *Rhiwnant* in earlier years, No. 35 survives and is waiting for restoration by South Coast Steam Ltd at Portland.

Pictured in the mid-1960s, S&L No. 59 heads south through Gretton Brook with a heavy ironstone train. One of the 56 class of nine powerful locomotives ordered by S&L to work their expanding network of Corby mineral lines, No. 59 was built by Robert Stephenson & Hawthorns (works No. 7670) in 1950.

Pictured in the mid-1960s, at Gretton Brook, S&L No. 59 pauses for discussion. A raised firebox specified by S&L made the class successful and free steaming. The 56 class used the same 4-foot diameter driving wheels as S&L's earlier Manning Wardle designs but were fitted with larger cylinders and a larger 180 psi boiler. With a tractive effort of 26,850 lbf, the 56 class were one of the most powerful industrial designs operating in the UK.

Pictured in the mid-1960s near Gretton Brook, S&L No. 53 stands in front of No. 48 *Criggion*. When Manning Wardle closed in 1926, their designs passed to Kitson & Co. *Criggion* was built by Kitson & Co. (works No. 5476) for S&L in 1936 to closely follow the pattern of S&L's earlier Manning Wardle locomotives. Kitson & Co. closed in 1938 and Robert Stephenson & Hawthorns acquired their drawings and goodwill. No. 53 was built in 1941 by Robert Stephenson & Hawthorns (works No. 7030) as a further continuation of the *c.* 1910 Manning Wardle design.

Having delivered its train to the ore reception sidings, S&L No. 59 has returned to rest beside No. 53 at Gretton Brook. Unfairly known as the 'Uglies', No. 59 and its class were withdrawn in 1969 when diesel traction became available. Although No. 59 was lost to scrap, five class members survive on heritage lines.

Middleton Towers and Leziate Works

The village of Sandringham shares its name with the Queen's North Norfolk estate and with the Sandringham Sands, rich deposits of quartz silica sand laid down in the Lower Cretaceous period. Since medieval times, sand from the parishes of Bawsey and Leziate, near King's Lynn, has been valued for glassmaking. Today, Norfolk produces sixty per cent of Britain's glass-making sand with a still-thriving industry that can trace its roots to the entrepreneurial spirit of Joseph Boam.

Railways reached the Bawsey area in 1846 with the opening of Middleton (later Middleton Towers) station. Quarrying was recorded in the area as early as the 1860s. Joseph Boam & Sons was formed in 1891. From 1881 a siding to the west of the station was being used for the sand trade, with a 3-foot gauge tramway in operation from 1884 to 1905. From 1904 a new siding was in operation to the east of the station with 1-foot 11½-inch gauge tramways in use from 1919. In the early 1900s, a processing plant had been built and the quarry extended to more than 500 acres. A 1951 merger with the Standard Brick & Sand Co. of Redhill led to the formation of British Industrial Sand Ltd (BIS).

John Dixon Abbott patented a reversing gearbox for motor trams in 1909. In 1911, with his father and brother, Abbott formed The Motor Rail & Tramcar Co. Ltd. Responding to a tender from the War Department, Motor Rail supplied more than 900 Trench Tractors during the First World War. Fitted with Dorman two-cylinder petrol engines and designed for 600 mm battlefield railways, Motor Rail's Trench Tractors were a reliable and effective alternative to horses and small steam locomotives. When Joseph Boam & Sons started building their tramway, Motor Rail's Simplex would have been a natural choice. Their first two Simplex locomotives were civilian versions of the Trench Tractor, built new for the quarry in 1919.

By the early 1960s, BIS operated a fleet of 4-wheel diesel locomotives on the Leziate narrow gauge system, twenty from Motor Rail and four from Ruston & Hornsby. On the standard gauge siding near Middleton Towers, BIS operated several small Motor Rail petrol- and diesel-powered locomotives and two steam locomotives. Peckett class M5 0-4-0ST (works No. 1874 of 1936) arrived from Redhill in 1954 after being purchased from Vauxhall Motors. 0-6-0ST works No. 1640 *Peter*, arrived in 1955. *Peter* was built by Hudswell Clark in 1929 for Sir Lindsay Parkinson & Co. Ltd civil engineers. Possibly named after Lindsay Parkinson's grandson Peter Parkinson, *Peter* was owned by the West Norfolk Farmers' Manure and Chemical Co-operative Co. from 1935 until its sale to BIS. Sadly, both locomotives were dismantled for scrap in 1963.

Middleton Towers station and the route to Swaffham closed in 1968. The line north from Middleton Towers to King's Lynn has remained open for sand traffic. Conveyers were added to the quarry in 1969 with some tramway lines remaining for spoil removal until 1977. The dramatic landscape around Leziate has been used as a filming location. Standing in for the North African desert, the quarry appeared in the 1970 *Dad's Army* episode 'The Two and a Half Feathers'. Since 2000, the quarry and sand refinery at Leziate have been owned by Sibelco. More than 700,000 tons are extracted annually, with the majority still transported by rail to UK glass factories. Lakes at Bawsey Country Park have been formed from flooded workings, beautifully restored for nature and recreation.

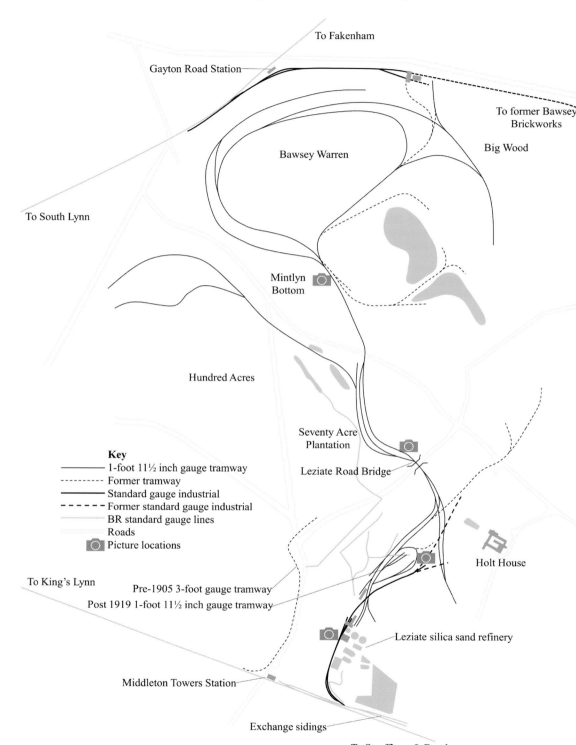

To Fakenham

Gayton Road Station

To former Bawsey
Brickworks

Big Wood

Bawsey Warren

To South Lynn

Mintlyn
Bottom

Hundred Acres

Seventy Acre
Plantation

Key

────── 1-foot 11½ inch gauge tramway
------ Former tramway
━━━━━━ Standard gauge industrial
━ ━ ━ ━ Former standard gauge industrial
────── BR standard gauge lines
　　　　 Roads
　◉　 Picture locations

Leziate Road Bridge

Holt House

To King's Lynn

Pre-1905 3-foot gauge tramway

Post 1919 1-foot 11½ inch gauge tramway

Leziate silica sand refinery

Middleton Towers Station

Exchange sidings

To Swaffham & Dereham

Above: Looking north towards Bawsey Warren in 1960. British Industrial Sand (BIS) No. 9 heads a train of sand skips on the narrow gauge tramway towards the Leziate sand refinery. Motor Rail Simplex No. 9 (Works No. 5696) was a 25/36hp model built in 1937. It served at BIS Redhill before arriving at Middleton in 1952. The scene is now completely under water and part of the Bawsey Country Park. (A. W. E. Hoskins, D. C. Pearce collection)

Right: BIS No. 17 pauses beside Leziate Road (Station Road) bridge. A visiting group of enthusiasts take a closer look at Motor Rail Simplex 20/28 hp No. 17 (works No. 8758). Pictured in 1961, No. 17 had been purchased new by BIS in 1942. Signal colour lights are visible above the bridge arch.

Hudswell Clarke Standard Contractors loco (works No. 1640) *Peter* stored in a siding north-east of the Leziate refinery, 1961. Built in 1929 and purchased by BIS in 1955, *Peter* had its cab and chimney cut down to work under sand loading gantries. From 1960 its leading coupling rods were removed, perhaps to help negotiate tighter curves.

Peckett class M5 (works No. 1874) pictured close to the Leziate refinery in 1961. Built in 1936 and acquired by BIS in 1954, No. 1874 served at BIS Redhill site before being moved to work near Middleton Towers. Like *Peter*, No. 1874 had its cab and chimney height reduced to clear overhead sand-loading equipment.

Wissington Light Railway

Wissington is the site of Europe's largest sugar beet plant. Each year, 3 million tons of beet are processed into 400,000 tons of sugar and 64,000 tons of biofuel, with waste energy used to heat the UK's largest green house. The modern plant depends on dozens of trucks arriving and departing each day. When it opened in 1925, the factory depended on light rail. There were no roads to Wissington. Although it was sugar that made a success of the Wissington Light Railway, its fragile economic foundations were built on horse feed and fertilizer dreams.

Railways reached Abbey, north of the Wissey, in 1882 with the Downham and Stoke Ferry Railway (D&SF). In 1904 Arthur James Keeble acquired 7,000 acres of land south of the Wissey. With his brother, Keeble had built up successful agricultural and brickmaking businesses in the Peterborough area. As an entrepreneur, Keeble recognised the potential of the fen's nitrogen rich peat for fertilizer making. With loans, he established an experimental ammonium sulphate works on the south bank of the Wissey. Keeble funded drainage projects, divided his land into small holdings and gave a name to Wissington. While celery, potatoes, carrots and even tobacco crops were attempted, hay for London tram horses became the main successful crop. Keeble's estate had poor road access but by 1906 railways were moving workers, crops, and materials. A horse tramway carried peat along the south bank of the Wissey to the ammonia works. With the help of the engineer John Grice Statter, the Wissey had been bridged, and a light railway operated south from the D&SF at Abbey to a terminus near Poppylot.

Sadly, 1906 was also the year that cold business reality arrived at Keeble's estate. Keeble Brothers Ltd went into receivership. The ammonia works needed more investment to achieve viability. The patience of his bankers had been tested to its limit. Fighting for his businesses and his land, Keeble found himself on the losing side of acrimonious legal disputes with his creditors. His debts had become a mortgage and, as the bank took over the estate, Keeble became a paying tenant on his former land. For Keeble, a tenacious visionary, the battles and the slide into bankruptcy must have been unimaginably stressful. In 1914, aged just fifty-eight, Keeble suffered a brain haemorrhage and died five days later.

Damaged by flooding, the light railway slid into disrepair. Its rescue came at the hands of a nearby landowner William Abel Towler. Encouraged by the Sugar Beet Subsidy Act, he formed British Sugar Manufacturing Ltd (BSM) and engaged McAlpine to build the plant at Wissington in 1925. The new factory was built around specialised processing equipment from Skoda in Czechoslovakia. Towler secured a £2,500 loan from the LNER to repair and extend Keeble's light railway, which grew in the 1920s to 18 miles, thirty loading points and 100 railway wagons.

As part of wartime efforts to increase food production, the Ministry of Agriculture (MoA) took over the running of the line in 1941, and for the first time the network became known as the Wissington Light Railway (WLR). In 1943, the first roads arrived at Wissington. With improving road transport, the railway south of the factory closed in 1957. As late as the 1970s, the WLR to Abbey was used for coke, lime, bulk sugar, molasses and animal feed traffic to and from the factory. The last train of beet pulp nuts ran in December 1981 and the WLR was sadly closed.

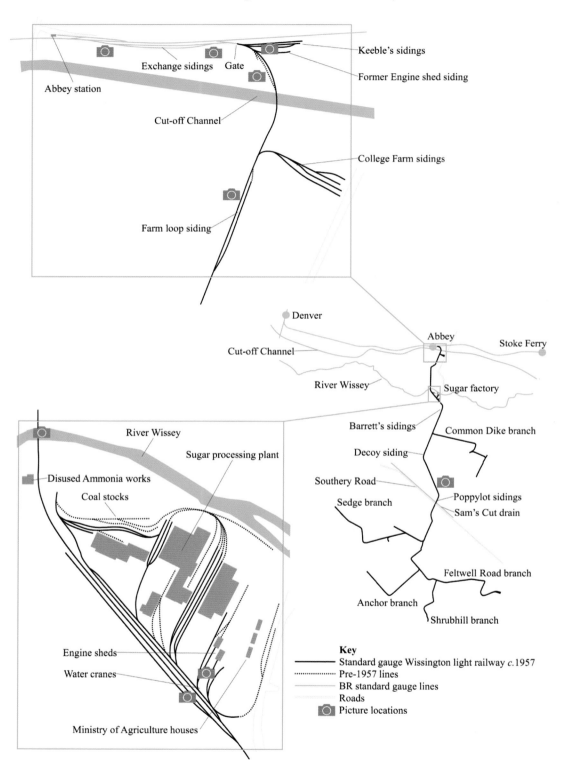

Above: Heading south on the WLR (Wissington Light Railway) *c.* 1955. With rails ahead obscured by grass and wildflowers, Hudswell Clarke 0-6-0ST *Hayle* forges bunker-first across the fenlands. It was not unusual for the crew to drop down from the footplate to rummage in the long grass to locate point levers for a siding or loop.

Right: A view from the footplate of *Hayle* heading north across the fens *c.* 1955. The rails ahead are just visible through the grass. The tree ahead has been shaped by the prevailing westerly wind. WLR lines south of the sugar factory sadly closed in 1957.

Pictured *c.* 1955, *Hayle*, its crew and the WLR Manager pose near the water crane. Built in 1924 by Hudswell Clarke for use in the construction industry, *Hayle* (works No. 1539) was acquired by the Ministry of Agriculture *c.* 1945 for use at Wissington. The large hose running over the smokebox was part of a water lifter to refill the saddle tank from streams and drainage channels. Renamed *Derek Crouch*, *Hayle* has been preserved on the Nene Valley Railway.

Pictured *c.* 1955 with a boiler feed pipe removed, *Mac* rests on a siding to the south of the factory. Built in 1899 by Hudswell Clarke (works No. 533), *Mac* was one of two locomotives used by McAlpine for the 1925 Wissington sugar factory construction project. When building work was complete, *Mac* stayed on as a works shunter. She was sadly sold for scrap in 1957.

Looking south from the factory *c.* 1955, *Ellesmere* rests in the foreground, while *Newcastle* stands in the distance on the left. *Ellesmere* was built by Barclay in 1908 (works No. 1158) and used on construction projects including the Rosyth naval base and the Gretna munitions factory. She was purchased for use around the sugar factory in 1926.

Locomotive maintenance on the WLR *c.* 1955. *Ellesmere* is supported by wooden blocks south of the factory with wheel-sets removed for repair. In 1957 *Ellesmere* was moved to the BSC (British Sugar Corporation) Selby plant as a spare locomotive. Sadly she was scrapped in 1965.

Above: Hudswell Clark 0-6-0ST (works No. 1700) *Wissington* at rest by the locomotive shed south of the factory in the late 1950s. *Wissington* was built for the BSC in 1938, and apart from an assignment to Spalding from 1945 to 1956, it spent its entire working life on the WLR. Although seldom steamed after 1970, when withdrawn in 1978 she was East Anglia's last industrial steam locomotive. *Wissington* is preserved on the North Norfolk Railway.

Left: The view south from the River Wissey bridge. Pictured in 1965, the remains of Keeble's 1905–1918 ammonia plant are still visible on the right. The 70-foot Wissey bridge and viaduct was built in 1905 to the design of Keeble's railway engineer, John Grice Statter. The sugar factory is out of frame to the left.

Pictured in 1965, *Newcastle* pauses close to the set of points that had been removed to convert Farm Loop into a siding. The meandering lines of the WLR were built with flat-bottom rails spiked to wooden sleepers with little or no ballast. *Newcastle* was built in 1901 by Manning Wardle (works No. 1532) for the Midland Coal Coke & Iron Co. of Apedale, Newcastle-under-Lyme. Its original open cab had been replaced by the time she arrived at the WLR in 1952. A bunker extension added in 1957 provided more fuel for long days working on the fens.

Pictured in 1965, *Newcastle* heads north towards Abbey across the Cut-off Channel bridge. Part of the extensive Fens drainage system, the Cut-off Channel runs for 28 miles from Barton Mills on the River Lark to Denver. Flood water from the River Lark, River Wissey and Little Ouse flow along the Cut-off Channel to the Denver Sluice and the Great Ouse. The bridge was built *c.* 1964 and still stands as a reminder of the WLR.

Newcastle continues north around the curve towards Abbey. Pictured in 1965, the passing loop that once followed the line of the curve is no longer visible. When the line was opened in 1905, a platform close to this location was used by farm workers and their families. Passengers leaving the light railway would walk the short distance to Abbey station to catch a train to nearby market towns. A small engine shed once stood beyond the trees. Like many of the locomotives on the WLR, *Newcastle* had a wooden barrier in the left-hand cab doorway to provide protection from the prevailing westerly winds.

Keeble's sidings looking east in 1965, *Newcastle* poses in the lush undergrowth typical of the WLR. On the footplate, Bill Harvey enjoys a day out from his normal duties as Norwich Shed Master. To reduce the risk of wildfires, the locomotives of the WLR were fitted with chimney top spark arresters. Close to Abbey, Keeble's sidings were named after Arthur James Keeble, the entrepreneurial founder of the Light Railway.

The lines of the WLR were laid with flatbottom rail spiked to wooden sleepers. As *Newcastle* heads beneath the arm of a loading gauge and through the WLR boundary gate, she moves onto the more heavily laid lines of BR with more conventional bullhead rail and cast iron chairs. The WLR mess hut is visible on the left. *Newcastle* was withdrawn in 1969 and sold for scrap in 1971. Fortunately, she was rescued and moved to South Cambridgeshire Railway in 1972. Today she can be seen at the Beamish Museum.

Richard Garrett Engineering
Leiston Works

As a division of Beyer Peacock, in the 1960s, Richard Garrett Engineering (RGE) was still the thriving heart of Leiston. With an entrepreneurial spirit and skills honed over generations, a committed workforce was able to take on almost any production challenge. Contract manufacturing kept the factory busy with projects including railway locomotive subassembly and production for Elliott shaping machines.

The works took their name from Richard Garrett, who started a farm machinery business in 1778. By the late 1840s Richard Garrett & Sons was a leading maker of stationary steam engines, expanding and diversifying with steam traction engines, road rollers and steam lorries. As early as 1913, Garrett were battery electric vehicle pioneers and in 1928 made some of the first experimental diesel engine road vehicles.

Railways reached Leiston in 1859 and in 1929 Aveling & Porter *Sirapite* replaced horses on Garrett's private siding. Once competitors, after the First World War, Aveling & Porter and Richard Garrett had been grouped under the same Agricultural & General Engineers (AGE) holding company. *Sirapite* had been built in 1906 for Gypsum Mines, and named after Sirapite plaster of Paris – an anagram of Parisite. AGE collapsed in 1932 and RGE became part of Beyer Peacock. With the closure of Beyer Peacock's Bowesfield joint-venture site, Electromobile W247 was relocated to Leiston in 1962 to replace *Sirapite*.

Garrett's private siding closed in 1968. RGE outlived much of Beyer Peacock, but sadly in 1981, the works closed. The 1852 Long Shop where Richard Garrett III pioneered flow-line production has become the centre of a fascinating museum. *Sirapite* is lovingly maintained by dedicated volunteers on the Leiston Works Railway.

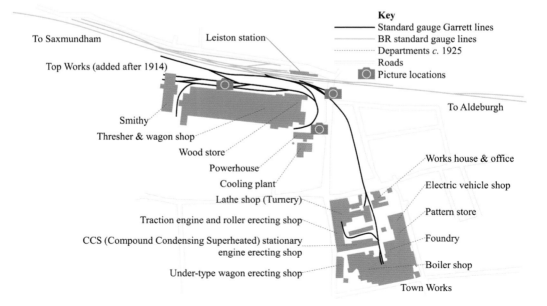

Key
— Standard gauge Garrett lines
— BR standard gauge lines
········· Departments *c.* 1925
Roads
◎ Picture locations

To Saxmundham

Leiston station

Top Works (added after 1914)

To Aldeburgh

Smithy
Thresher & wagon shop
Wood store
Powerhouse
Cooling plant
Lathe shop (Turnery)
Traction engine and roller erecting shop
CCS (Compound Condensing Superheated) stationary
engine erecting shop
Under-type wagon erecting shop

Works house & office
Electric vehicle shop
Pattern store
Foundry
Boiler shop
Town Works

Leiston station looking north-west from the Station Road level crossing *c.* 1963. The siding running to the left leads to the Top Works. The line running towards the camera in the left foreground leads to the Town Works. Although the station closed in 1966, the platform and some of the buildings are still visible today. The line through Leiston remains in place to serve Sizewell nuclear power station.

Sirapite pictured *c.* 1963 to the north of the Top Works. Built by Aveling & Porter (works No. 6158) in 1906 for Gypsum Mines Ltd, *Sirapite* arrived at Leiston in 1929 to replace Suffolk Punch horses working Richard Garrett & Sons' private siding. The Aveling & Porter Invicta prancing horse badge was replaced by a lioness, symbolising the defining qualities of Garrett's road locomotives: strength, silence and speed.

Sirapite, like other Aveling & Porter shunting locomotives, resembled a road traction engine. A horizontal two-cylinder compound steam engine was connected to the driving wheels by gears. Pictured *c.* 1963, *Sirapite* is happily preserved and can still be seen running at Leiston.

In 1962 *Sirapite* retired and was replaced a Battery Electric shunter. Pictured *c.* 1963, renovated and repainted, No. W247 had been built in the 1927 by Electromobile Ltd for use at Shoeburyness Artillery Range. A charging cable runs towards the Leiston Works powerhouse out of frame on the left.

Bowater's Railway

Spanning 3½ miles of the North Kent flatlands, the Bowater's railway linked Ridham dock on the River Swale with paper mills at Kemsley and Sittingbourne. Day and night, 2-foot 6-inch gauge steam locomotives shuttled the pulp, clay, paper and employees needed to maintain production. Founded with Frank Lloyd's 1904 horse-drawn tramway, when the line closed in 1969, it was the last industrial narrow gauge steam railway operating in the UK.

Local clay, limestone and abundant supplies of water made Sittingbourne a natural centre for brick, cement and papermaking. As early as 1708, Peter Archer was making paper in the area and from *c.* 1769 a paper mill was operating at Sittingbourne. Frank's father, Edward Lloyd, was one of the leading newspaper owners and publishers of the 1800s. The *Daily Chronicle* and *Lloyd's Weekly Newspaper* were bestsellers. His 'penny dreadful' books introduced Sweeney Todd to a blood thirsty audience. Seizing the opportunity to own more of his supply chain, in 1859 Edward acquired the lease on a paper mill site at London's Bow Bridge and by 1863 purchased the mill at Sittingbourne. When his father died in 1890, Frank Lloyd took over the running of the Edward Lloyd Ltd papermaking business. A horse-drawn tramway was built in 1904 to connect the papermill at Sittingbourne to barges at a new wharf on Milton Creek. *Premier* and *Leader*, the line's first two steam locomotives, were delivered in 1905. By 1912 the Sittingbourne Mill was the largest producer of newsprint paper in the world, supplying Fleet Street with over 100,000 tons per year.

Silt in the tidal waters of Milton Creek made it impractical for large vessels. In 1913 Edward Lloyd Ltd began work on a new dock on the Swale estuary. Ridham Dock would allow seagoing ships to service the Sittingbourne mill via an extension to the company's narrow gauge railway. With the outbreak of the First World War, the Admiralty took over the incomplete dock and railway. By 1916, trains could run over a new half-mile concrete viaduct at Sittingbourne, across Kemsley Down and into Ridham Dock. Completed in 1919, the dock was released by the Admiralty in 1922. The Roaring Twenties drove an ever-increasing demand for paper. In 1924, a new and enormous mill was opened on Kemsley Down. Under Frank Lloyd's leadership, the new village of Kemsley was built near the plant to provide homes for an expanding workforce.

Frank Lloyd's death in 1936 created an opportunity for the consolidation of the UK papermaking industry. Bowater acquired Lloyd's paper-making interests forming Bowater-Lloyd, a company that controlled 60 per cent of the UK newsprint market. At its peak, the Bowater-Lloyd narrow gauge system operated approximately 400 items of rolling stock, eleven steam locomotives, two fireless steam, one battery electric and one diesel locomotive. Standard gauge sidings were operated by two steam locomotives. An aerial cable-way carried logs from Ridham Dock to Kemsley mill. When economics caught up with the railway in 1969, the Locomotive Club of Great Britain was ready to take over operation as a preservation venture. Some of the railway's assets were used to construct the Great Whipsnade Railway. The southern part of the narrow gauge main line is preserved and operated as the Sittingbourne & Kemsley Light Railway.

The Sittingbourne mill closed in 2007 with much of the site being redeveloped as a supermarket. After ownership changes and significant investment, the Kemsley mill is making a thriving contribution to recycling. As Europe's second largest recovered fibre paper operation, it has an annual production capacity of 800,000 tons.

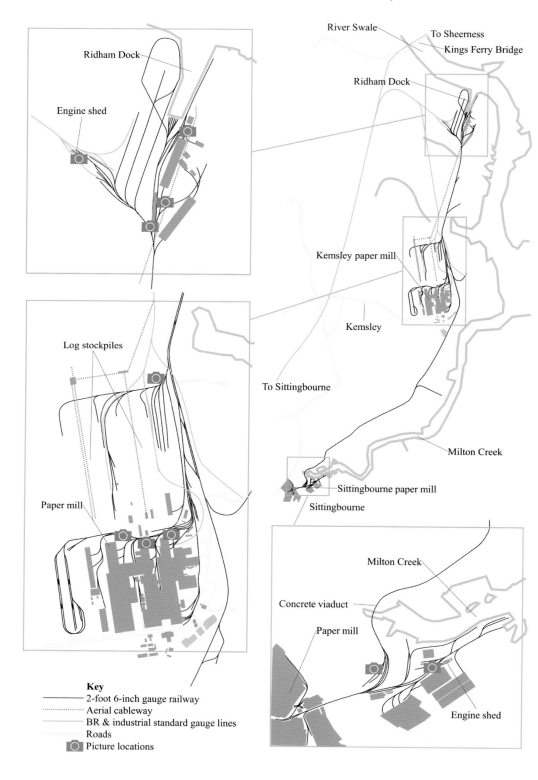

Ridham Dock

Engine shed

River Swale

To Sheerness

Kings Ferry Bridge

Ridham Dock

Kemsley paper mill

Kemsley

To Sittingbourne

Log stockpiles

Paper mill

Milton Creek

Sittingbourne paper mill

Sittingbourne

Milton Creek

Concrete viaduct

Paper mill

Engine shed

Key

—— 2-foot 6-inch gauge railway

········· Aerial cableway

—— BR & industrial standard gauge lines

Roads

Picture locations

Looking east towards Ridham Dock *c.* 1964, 0-6-0T *Pioneer II* stands in front of cranes and loading hoists. *Pioneer II* was at home on the exchange sidings near the dock. While still part of the BR fleet as No. 31178, she had been loaned to Bowater-Lloyd in 1953 and 1956. The former South Eastern & Chatham Railway class P was purchased by Bowater-Lloyd from British Railways (BR) in 1958.

Pioneer II beside Ridham Dock, looking north-west towards the Kingsferry lift bridge, *c.* 1964. Maintained in spotless condition, she was named after *Pioneer*, a Manning Wardle 0-4-0T that had been retired from Bowater's fleet in 1954. *Pioneer II* was sold in 1969 and has been preserved on the Bluebell Railway.

Bagnall 0-4-0ST *Jubilee*, works No. 2542, on exchange sidings near Ridham Dock, *c.* 1964. Named in celebration of the 1935 Silver Jubilee of King George V, *Jubilee* was purchased new in 1936 by Edward Lloyd Ltd in the same year that the company was acquired by Bowater. Until the arrival of diesel locomotives in the late 1960s, she shared duties on standard gauge sidings with *Pioneer II*. *Jubilee* has been preserved and can be seen today at the East Anglian Railway Museum.

0-4-4-0T *Monarch* shunts beside Ridham Dock. Cranes unload baled pulp from ships onto mountainous stacks. Named in celebration of Queen Elizabeth II, *Monarch* was built for Bowater by Bagnall in 1953 as works No. 3024. She was the last steam narrow gauge locomotive built for industrial service in the UK. With a Meyer 0-4-4-0T four-cylinder articulated configuration, and an unusual circular marine firebox, she was the most powerful locomotive built for the paper mill system. Bagnall built six similar locomotives for use on South African sugar estates.

Bagnall 0-6-2T *Superb* stands ahead of Manning Wardle 0-6-2T *Chevallier*. Fire was an ever-present risk around the docks and paper mills. Like many of the Bowater fleet, *Superb* is fitted with a diamond-shaped spark arrester. Pictured close to Ridham Dock, *c.* 1964, works No. 2624 *Superb* was built for Bowater-Lloyd in 1940 as a Bagnall continuation of the successful Kerr Stuart Barreto design. She is preserved today on the Sittingbourne & Kemsley Light Railway (SKLR).

Pictured *c.* 1964, close to Ridham Dock, Bagnall 0-6-2T *Conqueror* stands ready for its next duty ahead of a china clay hopper, *Superb* and *Chevallier*. Delivered in 1922 to Bowater predecessor Edward Lloyd Ltd, *Conqueror* was built by Bagnall as works No. 2192. After the closure of the paper mill line, she moved to the Great Whipsnade Railway in 1970. *Conqueror* is currently part of the Vale of Rheidol Museum collection.

With steam hissing from open cylinder cocks, *Chevallier* manoeuvres close to Ridham dock. *Chevallier* was built for the Chattenden & Upnor Railway in 1915 by Manning Wardle as works No. 1877. Pictured *c.* 1964, she had been purchased by Bowater-Lloyd in 1950. A tall dome, complete with antiquated Salter spring-balance safety valves sits between two boiler-top sand-pots. From 1970, *Chevallier* operated on the Great Whipsnade Railway and is currently preserved in private ownership.

North of the Kemsley paper mill, the narrow gauge main line ran parallel to what is now Fleet Road. Pictured *c.* 1964, three Bagnall locomotives are hard at work. *Superb* leaves the main line and crosses into the paper mill yard with a heavy train of pulp bales from Ridham Dock. In the centre, *Alpha* pauses. Northbound *Monarch* runs bunker-first with coaches from Sittingbourne to Ridham Dock. Trains ran twenty-four hours a day to move workers between sites.

Leaving the narrow gauge main line *c.* 1964, *Alpha* crosses the road and standard gauge siding and eases into the Kemsley mill yard. When Kerr Stuart closed in 1930, Bagnall recruited their chief draughtsman and other key staff members. *Alpha*, *Triumph* and *Superb* were built by Bagnall as a continuation of the successful Kerr Stuart 0-6-2T Barreto class. Oil canisters are kept warm near the smokebox.

Alpha runs south into the Kemsley yard with pulp bales for the mill, *c.* 1964. 0-6-2T *Alpha* was built for Edward Lloyd Ltd by Bagnall as works No. 2472 in 1932. When the Bowater-Lloyd narrow gauge line closed in 1969, *Alpha* passed into the hands of the SKLR where she is undergoing restoration.

Two fireless locomotives were used to shunt close to the paper mill buildings. Looking north, *c.* 1964, *Unique* gently draws empty pulp wagons away from the mill. 2-4-0F *Unique* was built by Bagnall for Edward Lloyd Ltd as works No. 2216 in 1924. She could operate for four to eight hours on each charge from Kemsley's 220 pounds per square inch steam plant. No. 2216 was the first of many fireless locomotives made by Bagnall. *Unique* is preserved as a static exhibit on the SKLR.

The second of the two Kemsley fireless locomotives *Victor* rests beside the northern wall of the paper mill. 0-4-0F *Victor* was built for Edward Lloyd Ltd. In 1929 as Bagnall works No. 2366. Pictured *c.* 1964, she was sadly scrapped in 1967.

Looking east, *c.* 1964, from a vantage point close to the northern wall of Kemsley paper mill. Fireless locomotive *Unique* has pulled pulp wagons away from the mill and runs into the head-shunt in the distance. In the foreground, *Alpha* picks up the empty train for the run back to Ridham dock.

Kemsley, *c.* 1964. 0-6-2T *Superior* shunts to the north of the mill. As the first of the Barreto class purchased by Edward Lloyd Ltd, *Superior* was built in 1920 by Kerr Stuart as works No. 4043. She has shorter side tanks and lacks the tall dome and diamond spark arrester fitted to the three Bagnall-built Barreto class locomotives. Originally equipped with unsuccessful oil burners, *Superior* was reboilered and converted to coal firing after just six months of service. The Kerr Stuart Matary design takes it nickname from the Barreto Company of Brazil who purchased the first of the class. In the background, tall pylons carry an aerial cable-way that was used to transport logs from Ridham dock to the mill. *Superior* is preserved on the Great Whipsnade Railway.

Bowater-Lloyd had impressive servicing facilities at the Kemsley mill. Pictured *c.* 1964, with its wheels removed, Barreto class 0-6-2T *Triumph* sits on wooden blocks. In the background, Brazil class 0-4-2T *Melior* is also under repair. *Triumph* was built by Bagnall in 1934 as works No. 2511. *Melior* was built by Kerr Stuart in 1924 as works No. 4219. Both locomotives were purchased new by Edward Lloyd Ltd, and both are preserved today on the SKLR.

Spare boilers under repair inside the servicing shop at Kemsley mill *c.* 1964. A third shorter boiler, possibly for the Brazil class locomotives, sits between the two longer boilers.

Looking east, *c.* 1964, from a vantage point close to the northern wall of Kemsley paper mill. Fireless locomotive *Unique* has pulled pulp wagons away from the mill and runs into the head-shunt in the distance. In the foreground, *Alpha* picks up the empty train for the run back to Ridham dock.

Kemsley, *c.* 1964. 0-6-2T *Superior* shunts to the north of the mill. As the first of the Barreto class purchased by Edward Lloyd Ltd, *Superior* was built in 1920 by Kerr Stuart as works No. 4043. She has shorter side tanks and lacks the tall dome and diamond spark arrester fitted to the three Bagnall-built Barreto class locomotives. Originally equipped with unsuccessful oil burners, *Superior* was reboilered and converted to coal firing after just six months of service. The Kerr Stuart Matary design takes it nickname from the Barreto Company of Brazil who purchased the first of the class. In the background, tall pylons carry an aerial cable-way that was used to transport logs from Ridham dock to the mill. *Superior* is preserved on the Great Whipsnade Railway.

Bowater-Lloyd had impressive servicing facilities at the Kemsley mill. Pictured *c.* 1964, with its wheels removed, Barreto class 0-6-2T *Triumph* sits on wooden blocks. In the background, Brazil class 0-4-2T *Melior* is also under repair. *Triumph* was built by Bagnall in 1934 as works No. 2511. *Melior* was built by Kerr Stuart in 1924 as works No. 4219. Both locomotives were purchased new by Edward Lloyd Ltd, and both are preserved today on the SKLR.

Spare boilers under repair inside the servicing shop at Kemsley mill *c.* 1964. A third shorter boiler, possibly for the Brazil class locomotives, sits between the two longer boilers.

Pictured *c.* 1964, *Premier* emerges from the shed at Sittingbourne. The first of four similar Kerr Stuart Brazil class locomotives built for Edward Lloyd Ltd, she was delivered in 1905 as works No. 886. *Premier* replaced horses on the narrow gauge lines between Milton Creek and the Sittingbourne paper mill. The class takes its name from earlier examples exported by Kerr Stuart to customers in Brazil.

Keen for its next duty, with safety valves blowing, *Leader* manoeuvres near the engine shed at Sittingbourne. Built in 1905, *Leader* (works No. 926) was the second Kerr Stuart Brazil class locomotive purchased by Edward Lloyd Ltd. Milton Creek is beyond the crane in the distance. *Leader* is preserved on the SKLR.

Sittingbourne, *c.* 1964. *Monarch*, the newest and most powerful steam locomotive operating on the Bowater narrow gauge system, stands in front of diminutive *Premier*, the first steam locomotive purchased for the line. The passenger coach behind *Monarch*, built on a pulp wagon chassis, was one of several used to shuttle Bowater employees to the mill and dock. *Monarch* was purchased in 1966 by the Welshpool & Llanfair Railway, where she can be seen today. *Premier* is preserved on the SKLR.

Vale of Rheidol Railway

Delighting tourists since 1902, the Vale of Rheidol Railway follows the contours of 11¾ miles of beautiful Welsh countryside between Aberystwyth and Devil's Bridge. Conceived to carry lead ore and timber for pit props, the 1-foot 11¾-inch gauge line along the south bank of the Afon Rheidol was engineered by Sir James Szlumper. Authorised by an 1897 Act of Parliament, a shortage of funds delayed construction until 1901. The line opened for freight in August and passengers in December 1902. Increasing tourism and a decline in lead mining meant that, almost from its opening, passenger traffic become the railway's main source of income.

In 1913, at a cost of just £27,311, a fraction of the project's £69,267 construction cost, the Vale of Rheidol Light Railway Company was absorbed into the Cambrian Railways (CR). During the First World War, with little tourism, the line served Army training camps and was sustained by an increase in timber traffic. As part of the CR, the Vale of Rheidol Railway was absorbed into the Great Western Railway in 1922. Closed during the Second World War, the line reopened in 1946 and became part of British Railways (BR) in 1948. From 1969 to 1989, it operated as the only steam-hauled line on the BR system. In 1989, the Vale of Rheidol Railway became one of the first parts of BR to be privatised. Today the line is a popular tourist attraction in the care of the Phyllis Rampton Narrow Gauge Railway Trust.

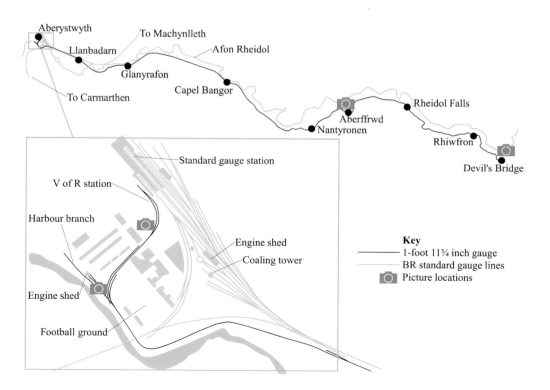

Aberystwyth, *c.* 1967. *Owain Glyndŵr* prepares to leave with a train for Devil's Bridge. No. 7 was introduced by the Great Western Railway (GWR) in 1923 as the first of three similar 2-6-2T locomotives built at Swindon for the Vale of Rheidol Railway. In *c.* 1956, she was named after Owain Glyndŵr, the Welsh independence leader who took Aberystwyth Castle in 1404. The Aberystwyth main line station is visible in the background. In 1968 the Vale of Rheidol moved into the former standard gauge platforms of the Carmarthen line at Aberystwyth.

With its right-hand coal bunker adorned with a snagged bouquet of foxgloves, *Llywelyn* joins its train at Aberystwyth. No. 8 was built at Swindon in 1923 and named in *c.* 1956 after the thirteenth-century prince of North Wales, Llywelyn the Great. *Llywelyn* and its classmate, No. 7, were built together to replace visually similar Davies Metcalf locomotives that had operated the line since its 1902 opening. The new locomotives were built with steam train heating that was removed during their early life. Pictured in the early 1960s, the train heating pipe bracket is still visible and being used as a convenient way to stow one of the safety chains.

Pictured *c.* 1959, with steam hissing from open cylinder cocks, No. 9 *Prince of Wales* backs onto its train. The GWR board had approved just two new locomotives for the Vale of Rheidol. With an act of skilful subterfuge, No. 9 was completed in 1924 as a third new locomotive. Swindon quietly scrapped Davies Metcalf No. 2 (GWR No. 1213) and presented the new locomotive as a rebuild. Building expenses were hidden as spare part costs. In 1948 the new No. 1213 became No. 9 and in *c.* 1956 inherited the name *Prince of Wales*, which had been carried by No. 2.

Aberystwyth Vale of Rheidol shed, *c.* 1965. No. 9 *Prince of Wales* simmers below the water tower. The houses in the background still stand on Greenfield Street, but the engine shed site has been redeveloped into a car park. In 1968 the Vale of Rheidol Railway moved into the vacated and refurbished standard gauge shed at Aberystwyth.

Part way from Aberystwyth to Devil's Bridge, No. 7 *Owain Glyndŵr* pauses to take water at Aberffrwd. Pictured *c.* 1967, Aberffrwd was operating with just a single line. An earlier passing loop was removed by British Railways after nationalisation. The station is almost unrecognisable today. The passing loop has been reinstated and, thanks to a 2013 European Union grant, raised platforms and new buildings have been added.

Devil's Bridge, the eastern terminus of the Vale of Rheidol Railway, viewed from the road bridge *c.* 1967. No. 7 *Owain Glyndŵr* prepares to depart for Aberystwyth. A coach and van stand by on the left to strengthen busy trains later in the day. The station building in the centre dates from 1902. Though updated, it remains today. On the far left, the black corrugated iron goods shed and two sidings have been removed. Though changed, the station's charm and spectacular rhododendrons remain today.

Devil's Bridge station in the early 1960s, looking west from the road bridge. No. 8 *Llywelyn* shunts its train back into the departure road. Unlike its two classmates, for much of its life *Llywelyn* ran with two sloping tool boxes behind the tank water filler covers.

No. 8 *Llywelyn* at Devil's Bridge in the early 1960s. Couplings and vacuum brake pipes are being secured. In the foreground, the curved bulge on the cab encloses the hand brake lever. The Vale of Rheidol Norwegian-style meat-chopper couplings and two safety chains are visible below. Weighing more than 25 tons, the three Swindon locomotives are the most powerful built to operate in the UK on 1-foot 11¾-inch gauge lines. *Llywelyn* and its classmates are preserved and still delight tourists on the Vale of Rheidol Railway.

Welshpool & Llanfair Railway

For more than fifty years, the people of Welshpool enjoyed the fascinating spectacle of steam locomotives threading trains between houses and along bustling streets. Opened in 1903, the 2-foot 6-inch gauge Welshpool & Llanfair Light Railway (W&L) linked the farming community of Llanfair Caereinion to the Cambrian main line station at Welshpool. Lossmaking and subsidised from its inception to its 1956 closure, the W&L served the community by moving people, coal, agricultural supplies and livestock across 8½ miles of picturesque Welsh countryside.

Railways arrived at Welshpool in 1860. Unsuccessful proposals to connect nearby Llanfair Caereinion into the Cambrian Railway (CR) via Meifod were made in 1865, and via Welshpool in 1864, 1877 and 1881. With support from local politicians, the Light Railways Act was passed in 1896 and enabled the release of treasury funds for railway projects. An official enquiry in 1896 chose a proposal for the W&L sponsored by William Addie, the mayor of Welshpool, over a competing route via Meifod.

With grants from the Treasury, contributions from local authorities and an agreement with the CR, the W&L project moved ahead as the first narrow gauge line in the UK enabled by the Light Railways Act. Under the terms of the CR agreement, signed in 1900, the W&L provided rolling stock and retained 40 per cent of revenue, and the CR constructed, maintained, and operated the line. Overcoming many financial and engineering challenges by April 1903 the W&L had received Board of Trade approval and ran its inaugural passenger service from Welshpool to Llanfair.

The W&L's first train was hauled by *The Countess*, the second of two 0-6-0T locomotives built for the line by Beyer Peacock in 1902. Along with its classmate, *The Earl*, it was named after the Earl and Countess of Powis. Edward Herbert (1818–1891), the 3rd Earl of Powis, had been actively engaged in the development of railway proposals. His nephew, George Charles Herbert (1862–1952), the 4th Earl of Powis, was a director of the W&L.

The CR was absorbed into the Great Western Railway (GWR) in early 1922. After further negotiation and an improved offer, the W&L was also purchased by the GWR. A GWR bus replaced passenger services on the line in 1931. In 1948 the W&L became part of British Railways (BR) with freight traffic continuing until closure in 1956.

Enthusiasts quickly began to explore ways to preserve the line and formed a society. The Welshpool & Llanfair Light Railway Preservation Company was formed in 1960. In 1961, *The Earl* and *The Countess* returned to the line from storage at Oswestry and coaches were acquired from the Chattenden & Upnor Admiralty line. A lease agreement was signed with BR in 1962 and by April 1963, trains were running between Llanfair Caereinion and Castle Caereinion. Occasional operation through the streets of Welshpool remained possible, but sadly ceased after the running of a last and commemorative double-headed train in August 1963.

Today, thanks to a dedicated team of enthusiasts, the W&L runs from Llanfair Caereinion to a new station at Raven Square on the outskirts of Welshpool. *The Earl* and *The Countess* are preserved in running condition. In Welshpool, traces of the former route can still be found. A bridge that carried the W&L across the Shropshire Union Canal still stands. The historic cattle dock beside Smithfield Road, with perhaps the only surviving example of dual gauge track in the UK, is being restored as a monument to Welshpool's railway heritage.

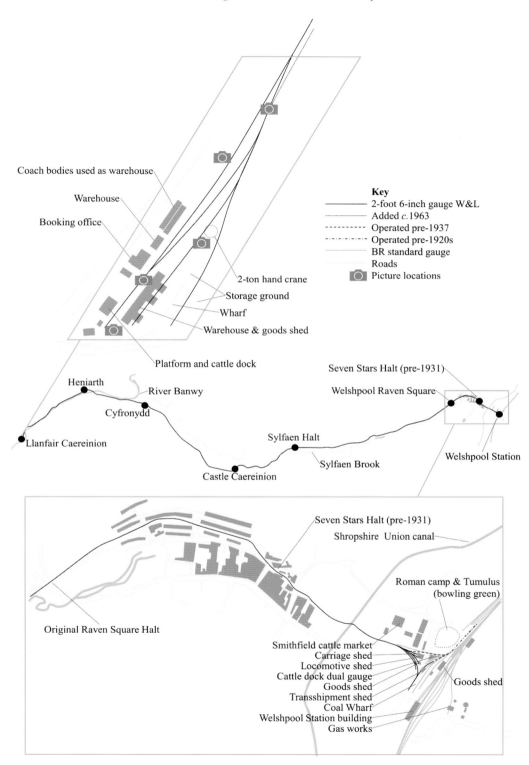

Llanfair Caereinion booking office *c.* 1964. Although the booking office was built with a front canopy and without chimneys, its basic structure dates from the opening of the Welshpool & Llanfair Light Railway (W&L) in 1903. The raised warehouse and Victorian coach bodies beyond the booking office were added before 1945, replacing a passenger seating area, and were used to increase covered farming supply storage at the station. Coal stocks are visible on the far right.

Looking north-west toward the Llanfair Caereinion goods shed. The booking office and warehouse are visible on the right. The goods shed was enlarged during its life and fitted with three canopies. Pictured *c.* 1964 only two remain. In the foreground, two 4-ton open wagons date from 1902 with Cambrian Railway modifications to replace rigid with sprung axle boxes, and new bodies fitted by the Great Western Railway (GWR). The green and white coach was acquired from the Chattenden & Upnor Railway, with doors fitted after its 1961 arrival. A W&L brake van stands beyond the coach. A cattle wagon is visible under the canopy.

The Earl rests beside the cattle dock at Llanfair Caereinion. *The Earl* was the first of two 0-6-0T locomotives built for the W&L in 1902 by Beyer Peacock (works No. 3496). Pictured *c.* 1964, *The Earl* has modifications that were fitted to both class members in the 1920s, including a larger dome, longer cab, boiler top-feeds, a new chimney and a characteristically GWR safety valve cover.

The Countess was the second of two locomotives built for the W&L in 1902 by Beyer Peacock (works No. 3497). Pictured *c.* 1964 to the east of Llanfair Caereinion station buildings, *The Countess*, unlike its classmate, retains the steam heating equipment fitted to both locomotives in 1925. The GWR converted both locomotives to right-hand drive but left the lever reverser in its original left-hand position. Test trains operated in 1902 had shown that wagons could become uncoupled on the steep gradients of the W&L. As a precaution safety chains were used beside the Norwegian-style meat-chopper couplings visible on the buffer beam.

The Earl and *The Countess* were named in honour of the Earl and Countess of Powis, who did much to encourage the building of the railway. A short boiler, outside frames and Walschaerts valve gear contributed to a sturdy design that could handle the steep climb to the line's 600-foot Sylfaen summit. The two locomotives shared duties on the W&L from its opening in 1903 to its BR closure in 1956.

Pictured, *c.* 1964, in early preservation, *The Countess* prepares to head out from Llanfair Caereinion. The former Admiralty officer/NCO 'Combination Car' in the foreground was one of the coaches acquired from the Chattenden & Upnor Railway in 1961. The lever frame and head shunt in the distance were added *c.* 1963.

Dinorwic Quarries (Padarn) Railway

The 7-mile Dinorwic Quarries Railway linked slate quarries near Llanberis to Port Dinorwic (Y Felinheli) on the North Wales coast. From the port, cut slate was sent to UK and world markets.

Commercial slate mining started near Llanberis in 1787 on land leased from Thomas Assheton Smith. From 1809 Assheton Smith and his son (also Thomas) took over the running of the quarry and drove a period of rapid expansion. Railways and inclines were operating in the quarry from 1812, and by 1824 a horse-drawn 2-foot gauge tramway reached the port. The tramway was a huge improvement over the packhorses it replaced, but its elevated route made it difficult to access slate from lower lying parts of the quarry.

In 1843, a new lakeside railway opened. Running along the banks of the Llyn Padarn, and known officially as the Dinorwic Quarries Railway, from its inception the line was known as the Padarn. In the early 1840s it may have seemed impractical to operate 2-foot gauge steam locomotives over long distances. The Padarn's 4-foot gauge gave the quarry owners confidence that they would succeed with steam traction and resulted in a most ingenious system. The quarry used wagons with double flange wheels on 1-foot 10¾-inch gauge track with nominally 2-foot rail centres. At Gilfach Ddu, quarry gauge wagons were loaded onto 4-foot gauge transporter wagons for the journey to Penscoins. Slate wagons were man-handled from the transporter wagons at Penscoins and lowered down an incline to Port Dinorwic and onto a network of quayside sidings.

When steam locomotives were available in 1848 to replace horses on the Padarn, the first, *Fire Queen*, shared a name with Assheton Smith's yacht. *Fire Queen* and its classmate *Jenny Lind* operated the Padarn until they were replaced from 1882 by *Dinorwic*, *Velinheli* and *Pandora*, the three Hunslet 0-6-0T locomotives that ran the line until its closure. *Dinorwic* (Dinorwig) and *Velinheli* (Y Felinheli) recognised villages at each end of the Padarn. *Pandora* shared its name with the yacht of Thomas's successor George William Duff. In 1904 George's brother, and Grand National winner, Charles Garden Duff inherited the quarry, and from 1904 many locomotives were renamed after racehorses. *Pandora* was renamed *Amalthæa* in 1909 perhaps continuing this theme. Workers travelled unofficially on the Padarn and from 1896 to 1947 carriages operated to formalise this practice.

Dinorwic quarries grew to encompass more than 700 acres across twenty gallery levels. At its peak in the late 1800s, more than 3,000 workers produced 100,000 tons per year. After Penrhyn, Dinorwic became the second largest slate quarry in the world. By the 1950s, waste tips within the quarry made extraction difficult. The Padarn sadly closed in 1961 but steam locomotives continued to operate on the gallery levels until at least 1968. A rock fall in 1966 paused production and by 1969 the quarry had closed.

The impressive 1871 workshops have become the National Slate Mining Museum. Many of the quarry's 1-foot 10¾-inch gauge engines have been preserved but sadly all three of the Padarn's 4-foot gauge Hunslet locomotives were lost to scrap. The remarkable 1848 *Fire Queen* and a director's saloon coach are preserved at the Penrhyn Castle Museum. The sole-surviving 4-foot gauge transporter wagon can be seen at the Narrow Gauge Railway Museum at Tywyn. Part of the Padarn's route has been used for the Llanberis Lake Railway. Port Dinorwic has become a smart marina. On Hen Gei Llechi, a slate chimney stands as a memorial to the port's industrial past.

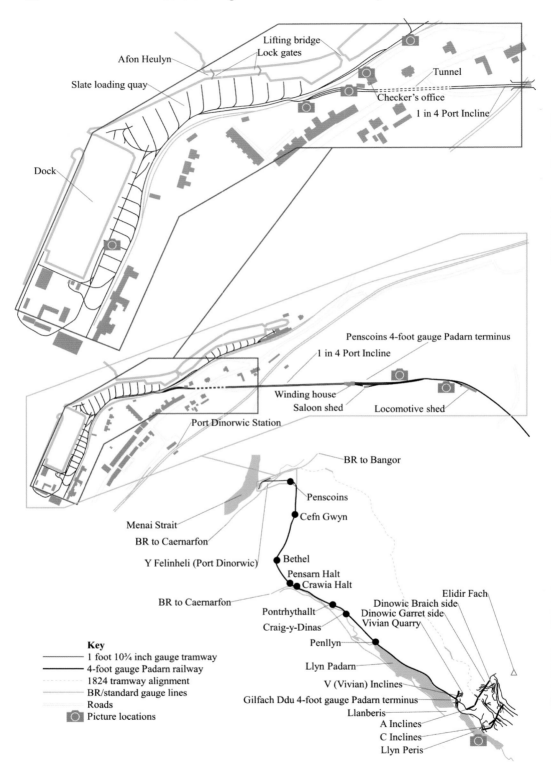

Lifting bridge
Lock gates
Afon Heulyn
Slate loading quay
Tunnel
Checker's office
1 in 4 Port Incline
Dock

Penscoins 4-foot gauge Padarn terminus
1 in 4 Port Incline
Winding house
Saloon shed
Locomotive shed
Port Dinorwic Station

BR to Bangor
Penscoins
Cefn Gwyn
Menai Strait
BR to Caernarfon
Y Felinheli (Port Dinorwic)
Bethel
Pensarn Halt
Crawia Halt
BR to Caernarfon
Elidir Fach
Dinowic Braich side
Dinowic Garret side
Pontrhythallt
Vivian Quarry
Craig-y-Dinas
Penllyn
Llyn Padarn
V (Vivian) Inclines
Gilfach Ddu 4-foot gauge Padarn terminus
Llanberis
A Inclines
C Inclines
Llyn Peris

Key
——— 1 foot 10¾ inch gauge tramway
——— 4-foot gauge Padarn railway
- - - - 1824 tramway alignment
——— BR/standard gauge lines
        Roads
📷 Picture locations

A *c.* 1959 view across Llyn Peris to the Braich (Branch) side of Dinorwic Quarry. The C1 incline rises to the winding house on the New York level. The ascent continues through C2 to C10 covering twenty gallery levels. A fleet of Hunslet steam and Ruston & Hornsby diesel locomotives worked more than 50 miles of internal quarry lines. The Lernion level above C8, 1,860 feet above sea level, had the UK's highest engine shed. The Garret side, Vivian, the Gilfach Ddu works and the start of the Padarn Railway are out of frame to the left.

Amalthæa, Hunslet 0-6-0T works No. 410 of 1909, approaches Penscoins after the 7-mile trip from Gilfach Ddu. *Amalthæa* is thought to be the only locomotive with the old English æ ligature in its name. Pictured *c.* 1959, the engine and carriage shed on the right is still standing in fields above Y Felinheli (Port Dinorwic).

Penscoins *c.* 1959 looking west towards the winding house above the Port Incline. 4-foot gauge Padarn transporter wagons each carried four 1-foot 10¾-inch quarry gauge slate wagons from Gilfach Ddu to Penscoins. Each load of four slate wagons was offloaded and lowered down the rope incline to the port, while empty wagons were raised to the winding house.

Pictured *c.* 1959 *Amalthæa* prepares to leave Penscoins for the journey back to Gilfach Ddu. The grey 'sentry box' on the right was loaded in place of one of the slate wagons and provided a bench seat and a rough ride for the brakeman. The shed on the left of the winding house had been used to store the luxurious four-wheeled director's saloon coach, used when the owners and their guests visited the quarry.

Right: The Hunslet locomotives of the Padarn were enthusiastic steamers. With its safety valves roaring under clouds of steam and smoke, *Amalthæa* heads towards Gilfach Ddu. In the foreground, some of the wagons are loaded with coal for the locomotives and stationary engines of the quarry.

Below: A view of the tunnel mouth at the foot of the Port Incline *c.* 1959. The point in the foreground is shaped for the double-flange wheels of the quarry gauge wagons. The canopy on the left may cover a weighbridge for checking the weight of each wagon. The Checker's Office, in the distance on the left, today forms part of a restaurant on Hen Gei Llechi, Y Felinheli (Port Dinorwic).

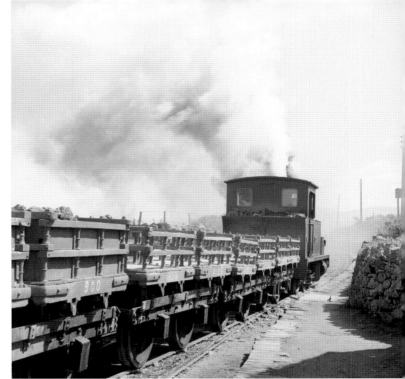

A short distance to the west of the Port Incline, the quarry gauge line crosses a standard gauge siding and connects to a network of lines along the quayside at Port Dinorwic. Pictured *c.* 1959, quarry gauge rails have been lifted while former LMS Fowler 3F 0-6-0T No. 47511 gently rolls along the siding.

Looking east at Port Dinorwic, close to the foot of the Port Incline, *c.* 1959. The British Rail standard gauge siding passes in front of the extensive network of quarry gauge lines along the quayside. Dinorwic Quarry No. A1, Ruston & Hornsby 30hp works No. 181807 of 1936, shunts slate wagons. No. A1 worked around the port from 1942 to 1961.

Dinorwic Quarries No. 1 shunts slate wagons in the curved sidings along the quayside. No. 1 was built by Hunslet as works No. 1429 in 1922. She was an early member of the Hunslet Port class and originally named *Lady Joan*. Pictured *c.* 1959, No. 1 was a popular Port Dinorwic character from 1922 until its 1963 assignment to the quarry.

No. 1 pauses in front of an unusually clean mineral wagon by Port Dinorwic dock, *c.* 1959. Today, Hen Gei Llechi (the Old Slate Quay) follows the route of the former dockside line. No. 1 has been preserved, renamed *Lady Joan* and can often be seen on the Bredgar & Wormshill Light Railway.

Penrhyn Quarry Railway

The 6-mile Penrhyn Quarry Railway (PQR) linked the Penrhyn slate quarry near Bethesda to Port Penrhyn on the North Wales coast. From the port, slate products were transported by sea and standard gauge rail to UK and world markets.

The 1-foot 10¾-inch gauge PQR opened in 1878, replacing and deviating from the route of its 1801 predecessor, the Penrhyn Railway (PR). The PR was itself inspired by, and extended, the route of the mile-long 1798 Llandegai Tramway, which linked a flint mill to the port. The Llandegai Tramway was one of the first railways in the UK and arguably the inspiration for the many railways around the world using a gauge of approximately 2 feet. The horse-drawn PR used a direct route with three balanced rope inclines. The meandering route of the PQR bypassed the three inclines and enabled uninterrupted steam locomotive operation from the foot of the quarry incline to Port Penrhyn. Using the 1-foot 10¾-inch 'quarry gauge' allowed single-flange locomotives and rolling stock to operate on the same track as double-flange vehicles designed for a 2-foot rail centre spacing.

Although slate had been quarried near Bethesda since medieval times, it was the Pennant family who capitalised the quarry business. From the 1770s Richard Pennant (later Baron Pennant of Penrhyn) and his steward William Williams industrialised extraction and introduced the gallery system of mining to work a large vein of slate at different heights. Felin Fawr (great mill) Slate Works was built a short distance to the north of the quarry, where the PR crossed a stream powerful enough to drive a waterwheel. In 1802, Felin Fawr used the world's first stone-cutting circular saw. At the peak of slate production in the late 1800s, Penrhyn quarry was the largest in the world with an annual output of more than 100,000 tons; 3,000 workers quarried, cut and transported slate from twenty galleries around a main pit nearly 1 mile across.

As PQR loads increased, more powerful locomotives were needed. In 1882 a large Hunslet 0-4-0ST *Charles* was ordered. The success of *Charles* led to the 1893 purchase of *Blanche* and *Linda*. The successful 0-4-0ST design is thought to have been influenced by Darjeeling A Class locomotives subcontracted to Hunslet. *Blanche* and *Linda* closely followed the design of *Charles* but were built with a slightly larger cylinder bore and higher boiler pressure. *Charles*, *Blanche* and *Linda* replaced three De Winton horizontal boiler locomotives and became the mainstay of the PQR main line. *Charles* was named after Charles Douglas-Pennant (1877–1914), the son of George Sholto Gordon Douglas-Pennant (2nd Baron Penrhyn). *Blanche* was named after the wife of Edward Sholto Douglas-Pennant (3rd Baron of Penrhyn), Blanche Georgina Fitzroy (1865–1944) and *Linda* after their daughter, Linda Blanche Douglas-Pennant (1889–1965).

Although the Welsh slate industry had been in decline since 1900, Penrhyn remained the largest and one of the most successful quarries. Overseas competition, a reduction in demand and improvements in road transportation sadly led to the closure of the PQR in 1962. Penrhyn is still operating as the UK's largest slate quarry but with a much-reduced workforce. Many historic buildings remain at Felin Fawr and Port Penhyn. Parts of the PQR can be explored on the Ogwen Trail. *Charles* can be seen at the Penrhyn Castle Railway Museum. *Blanche* and *Linda* are preserved on the Ffestiniog and many of the characterful locomotives that worked the galleries can still be seen on narrow gauge heritage railways across the UK.

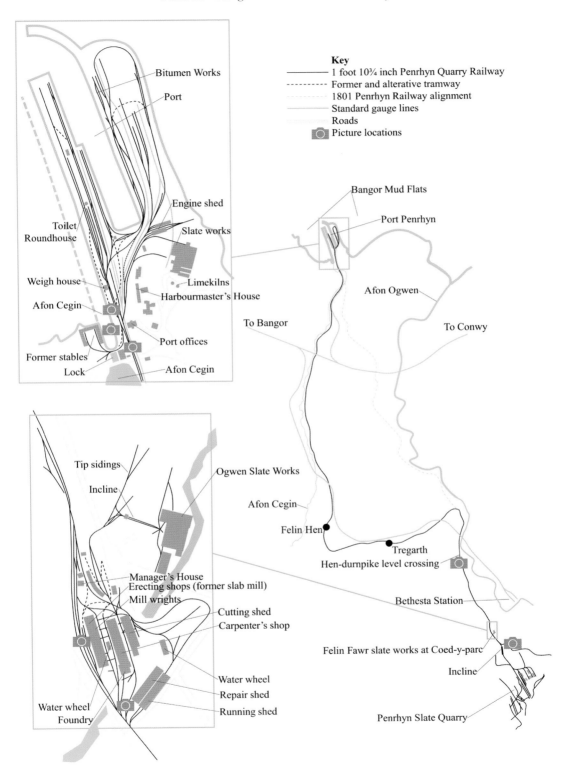

Key
— 1 foot 10¾ inch Penrhyn Quarry Railway
------ Former and alterative tramway
········ 1801 Penrhyn Railway alignment
— Standard gauge lines
········ Roads
📷 Picture locations

Bitumen Works

Port

Engine shed

Slate works

Toilet/
Roundhouse

Weigh house

Afon Cegin

Limekilns

Harbourmaster's House

Former stables

Lock

Port offices

Afon Cegin

Bangor Mud Flats

Port Penrhyn

Afon Ogwen

To Bangor

To Conwy

Tip sidings

Incline

Ogwen Slate Works

Afon Cegin

Felin Hen

Tregarth

Hen-durnpike level crossing

Manager's House
Erecting shops (former slab mill)
Mill wrights

Cutting shed
Carpenter's shop

Bethesta Station

Felin Fawr slate works at Coed-y-parc

Incline

Water wheel

Repair shed

Running shed

Water wheel
Foundry

Penrhyn Slate Quarry

Penrhyn Quarry, *c.* 1959. *Linda* shunts at ground level near the foot of the incline. The gallery levels above were worked by a fleet of four-wheel Ruston and Hornsby diesel engines and a few remaining Hunslet and Avonside steam locomotives. 0-4-0ST *Linda* was built for the quarry by Hunslet as works No. 590 in 1893.

Blanche rests by the locomotive shed at Felin Fawr (great mill) Slate Works, *c.* 1959. The shed and many of the other slate works buildings at Coed-y-Parc are still visible today. 0-4-0ST *Blanche* was built for the quarry by Hunslet as works No. 589 in 1893. *Blanche*, *Linda* and their 1882 classmate *Charles* ran the main line between the incline and Port Penrhyn.

As petrol and diesel displaced steam on the quarry galleries, a line of redundant locomotives formed beside the former slab mill at the Felin Fawr works. Pictured *c.* 1959 on the left, 0-4-0WT (well tank) *Eigiau* was built in Germany by Orenstein & Koppel as works No. 5668 of 1913. Kerr Stuart Tattoo class 0-4-2ST *Stanhope*, works No. 2395 of 1917, stands in the centre. To the right, vertical boiler 0-4-0 *Kathleen* dates from 1877 and was one of many De Winton locomotives to serve at Penrhyn.

Moving to the right along the charming but rusting line of characters, *Stanhope* and *Kathleen* are still visible on the far left. Manning Wardle 0-4-0ST works No. 1382 of 1897 *Jubilee 1897* stands ahead of Hudswell Clarke 0-6-0WT works No. 1643 of 1930 *Bronllwyd*. Pictured *c.* 1959, *Bronllwyd* had donated its boiler to another locomotive in 1951. Hunslet 0-4-0ST works No. 554 of 1891 *Lilla* stands in the centre. In the foreground *Edward Sholto* was built in 1909 as Hunslet works No. 996 and was the last steam locomotive to be bought new by the quarry.

Above: Continuing to the right, *Lilla* and *Edward Sholto* are still just in frame on the left. With bunker lining still shining in the sun, Hunslet 0-4-0ST works No. 995 of 1909 *Gertrude* stands ahead of Hunslet 0-4-0ST works No. 317 of 1883 *Lilian*. In the foreground 0-6-0T *Sgt. Murphy* was built by Kerr Stuart for the Admiralty as works No. 3117 in 1918 and purchased by the quarry in 1920. Miraculously, all of the locomotives in line at Coed-y-Parc *c.* 1959 have been preserved, and most are maintained in running condition.

Left: Heading north from Coed-y-Parc *c.* 1959 with no suspension, the slate train ride was bone shaking. Hunslet 0-4-0ST *Linda* slows as she approaches Hen-durnpike (old turnpike) level crossing. The crossing keeper's hut ahead of the train on the left still stands near Lon Hafoty and the B4409. Sadly the signal post and railway have vanished.

Right: The gated approach to Port Penrhyn, looking north, *c.* 1959. *Linda* takes water from the standpipe under the road bridge as she prepares to take a train of empty wagons back to the quarry. The signal may indicate open or closed gates. The standard gauge port siding is visible on the right. Although the rails have been lifted, the vantage point can be reached today on the Ogwen Trail cycle path.

Below: Port Penrhyn looking north from the road bridge *c.* 1959, *Blanche* shunts empty wagons. Today, the rails and the coal stocks in the distance have been removed, but the buildings remain. The Port Offices are on the right and the weigh house is in the distance on the left. The roundhouse in the far distance is a historically significant workers toilet. Dating from *c.* 1800, it may have been the first flush toilet in Bangor. Seating twelve, it's the largest communal facility in Wales.

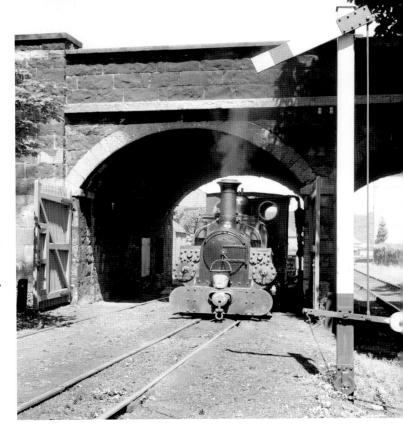

Port Penrhyn *c.* 1959, *Blanche* shunts a train of empty slate wagons beside the Port Offices. Although the locomotives and rolling stock were fitted with conventional single-flange wheels, the points at Port Penrhyn, and near the quarry, were designed for double-flange wheels. The white levers operate rods and cranks that move the rails at the toe of the stub-point and twist the angle of the rail at the heel where the frog would normally be located.

Pictured *c.* 1959, *Blanche* stands ready with a train of empty slate wagons to leave Port Penrhyn for the quarries. *Blanche* and *Linda* carried sand in the cylindrical boxes on the saddle tank front. Sand helped improve grip on slippery rails. The galvanized bucket by the smokebox, characteristically carried by the Penrhyn main line engines, contained extra sand.

Linda arrives at Port Penrhyn with a loaded train from the quarry. Pictured *c.* 1959, the wagons near the front of the train carry sacks of fullersite, ground waste slate used in the making of roofing felt and polishing powders. Large slate panels are loaded near the rear of the train, and two passengers are visible near the bridge.

Linda crosses over standard gauge sidings near the quayside at Port Penrhyn. The Harbourmaster's house is visible on the left, and an Austin 8 is on the right. Pictured *c.* 1959, *Blanche* and *Linda* were maintained in smart black livery until the Penrhyn Quarry Railway closed in 1962. Both are preserved, have been converted to 2-4-0, fitted with small tenders, and can often be seen running on the Ffestiniog Railway.

Talyllyn Railway

The 7¼-mile Talyllyn Railway opened in 1865 to connect the Bryn Eglwys Quarry, near Abergynolwyn, to the Cambrian main line at Tywyn. Built mainly for the conveyance of slate, the Talyllyn was also the first narrow gauge railway authorised by an Act of Parliament to operate steam-hauled passenger trains. In 1951, thanks to the inspiring leadership of Tom Rolt, the Talyllyn became the world's first volunteer-run heritage railway.

By a strange twist of fate, the Talyllyn Railway can trace its inception to the American Civil War. In 1859 Hengwrt Hall, near Dolgellau, was purchased by wealthy Lancashire mill owner William McConnel. The 1861 Civil War suspended cotton supplies, forcing McConnel to look for new business opportunities. In 1864, McConnel formed the Aberdovey Slate Company and took on the lease of the Bryn Eglwys quarry. With capital to invest, McConnel increased production, and by July 1864, started work on a railway to replace packhorses for slate transport. Taking its name from the hamlet of Talyllyn (meaning 'end of the lake'), the new route was surveyed and engineered by James Swinton Spooner. Following the practice of the nearby horse-drawn Corris Railway, and perhaps local quarry tradition, the line was built to a gauge of 2 feet 3 inches. Slate and passenger services started unofficially in 1865 with Board of Trade approval granted in 1866. Passenger services started between Pendre and Abergynolwyn, with Rhydyronen halt added in 1867, followed by Dolgoch and Brynglas.

Local landowner Henry Haydn (later Sir Haydn) Jones recognised the importance of slate to his community. When the quarry closed in 1910, Haydn Jones bought the business. Operation restarted in 1911 until rock falls in 1946 finally brought an end to safe working. Having made a promise to his community, Haydn Jones heroically managed to keep the railway running until his death in 1950 at the age of eighty-six. Thanks to the efforts and donations of volunteers and enthusiasts the Talyllyn reopened as a heritage line in 1951. Celebrating 150 years of service in 2015, the Talyllyn continues to be an inspiration for the preservation movement.

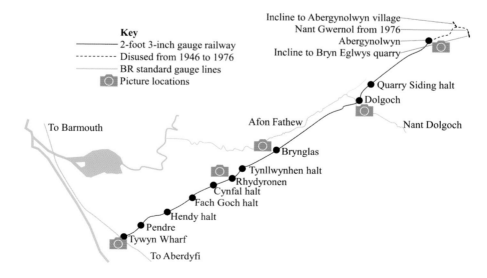

Key
- 2-foot 3-inch gauge railway
- Disused from 1946 to 1976
- BR standard gauge lines
- Picture locations

Incline to Abergynolwyn village
Nant Gwernol from 1976
Abergynolwyn
Incline to Bryn Eglwys quarry

Quarry Siding halt
Dolgoch

Afon Fathew   Nant Dolgoch

To Barmouth

Brynglas
Tynllwynhen halt
Rhydyronen
Cynfal halt
Fach Goch halt
Hendy halt
Pendre
Tywyn Wharf
To Aberdyfi

0-4-2ST No. 4 *Edward Thomas* prepares to leave Tywyn Wharf. No. 4 was built by Kerr Stuart for the Corris Railway as works No. 4047 in 1921. She was out of service and in need of overhaul when the Corris Railway was closed by BR in 1948. In 1951, for just £25, No. 4 was acquired by the Talyllyn preservation group and overhauled at no charge by the Hunslet Engine Company. Entering service in 1952, she was given the name *Edward Thomas* to honour the Talyllyn Railway's former manager. Pictured *c.* 1955, buffers and running plates have been recently fitted.

Edward Thomas eases away from Tywyn Wharf. Pictured *c.* 1955, the original Narrow Gauge Railway Museum building is under construction on the site of the former coal yard. The office on the right dates from 1866. The tall signal and road bridge in the distance mark the position of the Cambrian main line. Throughout its working life, the station operated as a fan of sidings. The run round loop and platform were added in 1952, shortly after the line was preserved and reopened. In the left foreground, the cab of former Welsh Highland Railway (WHR) locomotive *Russell* is just visible.

Tywyn Wharf *c.* 1961, 0-4-2T No. 1 *Talyllyn* has arrived with a train from Abergynolwyn. No. 1 was built for the Talyllyn Railway by Fletcher, Jennings & Co. as works No. 42 in 1864. Former WHR 2-6-2T *Russell* has been repainted and is displayed in the distance. *Russell* was built by Hunslet in 1906 as works No. 901. In 1965 she was passed back to the WHR preservation group and is currently maintained in running condition. Lines leading towards the camera are on a raised platform for slate transhipment to a standard gauge siding out of frame on the left. Wagon turntables connect the perpendicular lines.

Metre gauge 0-6-0T *Cambrai* on display at Tywyn *c.* 1961. *Cambrai* was built in 1888 by Paris-based Corpet-Louvet as works No. 493. Originally named *Clary*, she operated on the Chemin de fer du Cambrésis in northern France until 1936. Overhauled before sale, she gained the name and perhaps the side tanks of one of her stablemates. As *Cambrai* she worked on the Loddington Ironstone tramway in Northamptonshire until 1956 and the Waltham Iron Ore Tramway until 1960. She was rescued by the Narrow Gauge Railway Museum and arrived at Tywyn in late 1960. Unusually, *Cambrai* has outside Stephenson valve gear. She can be seen today at the Irchester Narrow Gauge Railway Museum.

Tywyn Wharf, *c.* 1967, No. 2 *Dolgoch* prepares to take the refreshments van forward to Abergynolwyn. *Dolgoch* was built for the Talyllyn Railway by Fletcher, Jennings & Co. in 1866 as works No. 63. Although she was delivered just two years after the railway's first locomotive, *Talyllyn*, she was built to a very different design. A stable long wheelbase 0-4-0WT (well tank) layout placed the rear axle behind the firebox. Inside Allan valve gear was driven from the leading axle. Until *Edward Thomas* arrived at the preserved Talyllyn Railway, *Dolgoch* was the line's heroic and only operating steam locomotive. *Dolgoch* was fully overhauled between 1954 and 1963. The decorative brass valves on the running plate above the buffers were once cylinder lubricators. They were replaced by a mechanical lubricator visible above the leading splasher.

Onlookers enjoy the *c.* 1967 theatre as No. 2 *Dolgoch* and No. 6 *Douglas* accelerate away from Tywyn Wharf. The leading coach, No. 17, served on the Corris Railway from 1898. From 1930 it was used as a garden summerhouse before being rescued and restored by the Talyllyn Railway in 1958.

No. 1 *Talyllyn* runs through charming Rhydyronen with a train for Tywyn. Pictured *c.* 1967, No. 1 has an unusual rigid 0-4-2ST layout. Trailing wheels were added in 1867, just two years after delivery, to cure the bouncing instability of its original 0-4-0ST arrangement.

No. 4 *Edward Thomas*, complete with Giesl exhaust ejector, heads east through Rhydyronen. Named after the nearby stream, Nant Rhyd-yr-onnen, and opened in 1867, Rhydyronen was the railway's first intermediate station. Pictured *c.* 1967, the passing loop was completely removed by 1977.

A busy day at Brynglas in the early 1960s. With outstretched arms, tokens are exchanged from westbound *Douglas* on the left and eastbound *Talyllyn* on the right. Brynglas was opened as a station in 1872 and named after a local farm. A goods siding was converted into a passing loop in 1953. The four lever frame was enclosed in a small hut in the late 1960s. The hut was enlarged and two more levers were fitted to control a siding added in 1975.

Built with slate blocks from the Bryn-Eglwys Quarry, the original water tower at Dolgoch dates from the line's 1865 opening. Though partly reclaimed by nature, it was still operational in this mid-1960s scene. The structure has been renovated today with a wooden chute replacing the hose. The new water tower in the distance was added in 1961. The platform on the left was built in 1867 and extended in 1961.

Above: Dolgoch, *c*. 1961. The falls' low roar refracts through the trees. A distant exhaust beat echoes along the valley. With an unmistakable glimpse of steam through the trees, a flash of green, *Edward Thomas* is on the viaduct.

Left: Pictured *c*. 1967, *Edward Thomas* speeds eastward over the viaduct into Dolgoch station. The spectacular three span brick viaduct crosses 57 feet above the Nant Dolgoch. Walking trails and waterfalls make Dolgoch a favourite destination for tourists. On perhaps the most magical railway, the view across the ravine at Dolgoch is, with little doubt, the most enchanting.

Right: No. 4 *Edward Thomas* takes water at Dolgoch. Pictured *c.* 1967, No. 4 is running with a Giesl ejector. The flattened blastpipe invented by Dr Giesl-Gieslingen was fitted to *Edward Thomas* in 1958. A claimed improvement in coal consumption was later disputed when the ejector was removed in 1969. The Giesl ejector is now part of a cut-away exhibit at the Narrow Gauge Railway Museum in Tywyn.

Below: Lineside to the east of Dolgoch, *c.* 1961. No. 4 *Edward Thomas* heads east towards Abergynolwyn.

Abergynolwyn *c.* 1955. No. 4 *Edward Thomas* has run round its train and prepares for the journey back to Tywyn. Abergynolwyn was the passenger terminus of the original Talyllyn Railway. A mineral line extended to the foot of the Alltwyllt incline and access to the Bryn Eglwys quarry. From 1976, the preserved line was extended over the path of the mineral line to a new eastern terminus at Nant Gwernol.

0-4-0WT No. 6 *Douglas* arrives at Abergynolwyn, *c.* 1967. The Barclay E class, works No. 1431, was built in 1918 for the Air Service Construction Corps and used on projects at RAF Manston and Calshot. In 1949 she was purchased by Abelson & Co., who presented her to the Talyllyn. Retubed and regauged from 2 feet to 2 feet 3 inches, and named after Douglas Abelson, she entered service in 1953. The refreshments van is visible on the right. In 1969, the 1930s slate station building was replaced and the station layout modified.

Festiniog Railway

The scenic 1-foot 11½-inch gauge line from Porthmadog to Blaenau Ffestiniog is operated by the Festiniog Railway (FR), the world's oldest independent railway company. Engineered by James Spooner, the 1 in 80 sloping route opened in 1836 as a gravity and horse-drawn tramway. Horses took nearly six hours to haul empty wagons 13½ miles uphill from port to quarry. Slate trains made the downhill trip in just ninety minutes, with horses riding in dandy wagons.

When Charles Easton Spooner (James' son) took control in 1856, it was clear that the line's capacity could be increased with faster uphill journeys. Steam had been introduced on the Padarn Railway in 1848, but its use on the narrow gauge of the FR would have seemed challenging. In 1863, George England & Co. delivered *Mountaineer*, *Princess* and *Palmerston*, followed months later by *Prince*. Together, they were the first truly successful narrow gauge locomotives. In 1864 the FR became the first narrow gauge railway in the world to run steam-hauled passenger trains. The application of Robert Fairlie's articulated double engine concept, beginning with *Little Wonder* in 1869, further increased capacity, with slate traffic eventually peaking at 130,000 tons per year. As late as 1939, slate trains with formations of eighty wagons were still worked downhill by gravity.

By the 1920s the FR depended more on tourism than its declining slate traffic. Passenger services were withdrawn in 1939 with slate traffic struggling on until 1946. In 1954, the FR was acquired by Alan Pegler and transferred to a charitable trust. Thanks to the dedication of volunteers, from 1955 the line steadily began to reopen, with trains reaching Tan-y-Bwlch in 1958. The flooding of the original route by the Tanygrisiau reservoir required the heroic construction of the 2½-mile Llyn Ystradau Deviation. In 1982, 150 years after the Festiniog Railway Company was founded, and to the delight of enthusiasts, trains once again ran from Porthmadog to Blaenau Ffestiniog.

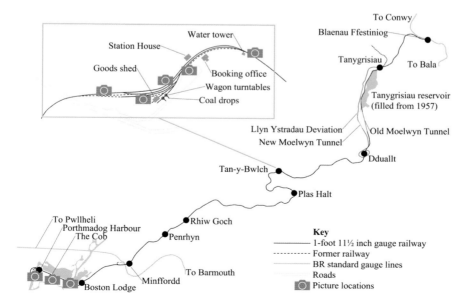

Porthmadog, *c.* 1958, 0-4-0ST+T No. 2 *Prince* prepares to leave for Tan-y-Bwlch. When the Festiniog Railway (FR) closed in 1946, *Prince* was being overhauled. Under preservation, she was the first locomotive returned to service in 1955. Honouring Albert Edward, Prince of Wales, No. 2 was built by George England in 1863, and was one of the first four locomotives delivered to replace horses on the FR.

George England 0-4-0ST+T No. 1 *Princess* as a static exhibit at Porthmadog *c.* 1963. In August 1863 No. 1 was the first steam locomotive to run on the FR. Poetically, in August 1946, she worked the last train before closure. Introduced with side tanks and an open cab, a late 1890s rebuild transformed the appearance of Nos 1 and 2 into almost the current form. Named in honour of Princess Alexandra of Denmark (later Queen Alexandra), No. 1 remains today as a roaming static exhibit.

Double Fairlie 0-4-4-0T No. 10 *Merddin Emrys* is being prepared at Porthmadog. Pictured *c.* 1963 with much of its cab missing, No. 10 had recently returned to service after boiler stay repairs. No. 10 was the third Double Fairlie designed by George Percival Spooner and the first to be built at Boston Lodge. The double-ended articulated concept was patented by Scottish engineer Robert Francis Fairlie in 1864. Introduced in 1879, No. 10 was named after the legendary Welsh wizard Merddin Emrys (Myrddin Emrys, or Merlin).

Surrounded by the generous undergrowth of the early preservation years *c.* 1958, recently reintroduced 0-4-4-0T No. 3 *Taliesin* simmers at Porthmadog. No. 3 was the fourth Double Fairlie designed by George Percival Spooner and the second to be built at Boston Lodge. Introduced in 1886 as *Livingston Thompson*, she was renamed *Taliesin* in 1932, taking on the name of a withdrawn Single Fairlie. From 1853 to 1874, Livingston Thompson was a leading member of the FR Company board. The Celtic poet Taliesin is fondly remembered as the Chief of Bards.

Pictured *c.* 1963, No. 3 *Earl of Merioneth* arrives at Porthmadog from Boston Lodge ready to head an afternoon departure. In honour of Prince Charles, No. 3 was renamed from *Taliesin* to *Earl of Merioneth* in 1961. After eighty-five years of service, she was withdrawn in 1971. Once more named *Livingston Thompson*, she is exhibited today at the National Railway Museum. Established in 1851, Britannia Foundry, in the background, was sadly demolished in 1972. The foundry made equipment and wagons for the slate industry.

Beautifully polished, Hunslet 0-4-0ST+T *Linda* prepares to leave Porthmadog. When the 1-foot 10¾-inch gauge Penrhyn Quarry Railway closed, *Blanche* and *Linda* were rescued and moved to the 1-foot 11½-inch gauge FR. Weeks after its 1962 arrival, and before being re-gauged, *Linda* derailed 5 miles from Porthmadog at a location that became known as Linda's Leap. Pictured *c.* 1966, *Linda* has been re-gauged, repainted, fitted with a tender, modified cab, vacuum brakes, larger sandboxes and chopper couplings.

Boston Lodge, the main works of the FR, *c.* 1966. Established in 1842, the FR works have become the oldest in the world still serving their original railway. In the distance, *Prince* stands beyond *Linda*, with 2-4-0 Diesel *Moelwyn* on their right. Boston Lodge takes its name from Boston in Lincolnshire, the parliamentary constituency of William Alexander Madocks, the agricultural improver who built the Cob and gave a name to Port Madoc (later Porthmadog).

Excited young passengers pose for the camera. No. 2 *Prince* gallops through the rock cutting at the approach to Tan-y-Bwlch. Pictured *c.* 1963, *Prince* is running with straight outside frames, fitted in 1962. A 1974 to 1980 overhaul reinstated the earlier stepped frame profile below the saddle tank.

Tan-y-Bwlch *c.* 1966. *Linda* arrives while *Blanche* waits to depart tender-first for Porthmadog. In later years, both locomotives were rebuilt from 0-4-0ST+T to 2-4-0ST+T. Tan-y-Bwlch opened in 1873, replacing the earlier station at nearby Hafod-y-Llyn. Under preservation, service was restored from Porthmadog to Tan-y-Bwlch by 1958. In 1968, the route opened beyond Tan-y-Bwlch to Dduallt, eventually reaching Blaenau Ffestiniog via the Llyn Ystradau Deviation in 1982.

A busy scene at Tan-y-Bwlch, still grass covered *c.* 1958. No. 2 *Prince* has run round its train and prepares for the return journey to Porthmadog. Bessie Jones, the station mistress, famous for wearing Welsh National Costume, hurries towards the station house. Bessie and her husband Will lived in the station house from 1924 until they retired in 1968. The wooden booking office on the right dates from *c.* 1873.

Above: Tan-y-Bwlch looking south-west. No. 2 *Prince* stands below a cloud of steam. The stone goods shed in the distance dates from 1883. Pictured *c.* 1958, the 1½-ton gibbet crane is visible beside the shed. The cart, near the shed, stands on the site of two wagon turntables that once served coal drops. Affectionately known as 'Bug Boxes', the four-wheel coach on the left dates from the 1860s. Today, a raised platform has been added and the goods shed converted into a café.

Right: As curious passengers look on, No. 2 *Prince* takes water at the east end of Tan-y-Bwlch, *c.* 1958. Although a larger water tower was built nearby in the 1980s, the plinth of the original remains today. The two cylindrical sand pots beside the smokebox are characteristic of FR locomotives. The coupling below the smokebox door includes a Norwegian-style chopper at the top and an underslung hook and link for compatibility with older rolling stock.

Ex-Penrhyn Quarry Railway 0-4-0ST *Linda* in beautiful condition stands on the cob near Porthmadog. Pictured *c.* 1966, newly built Observation Car No. 100 had been numbered in celebration of the FR 1865 to 1965 passenger centenary. Gleaming in the afternoon sun, *Linda* is a tribute to the skill and dedication of the many volunteers who brought the FR back to life.